Dear Gary,

Enjoy this book.

Your fiend,

Daniel Brichto

GW00498561

RITUAL SLAUGHTER

RITUAL
SLAUGHTER

SIDNEY BRICHTO

SINCLAIR-STEVENSON
LONDON
in association with the
European Jewish Publication Society
ejps

First published in the United Kingdom 2001
by Sinclair-Stevenson
3 South Terrace, London SW7 2TB

The European Jewish Publication Society to a
registered charity which gives grants to assist in the publication
and distribution of books relevant to Jewish literature,
history, religion, philosophy, politics and culture

ISBN 0 9540476 1 3

Typeset by Rowland Phototypesetting Ltd,
Bury St Edmunds, Suffolk
Printed and bound in the United Kingdom by
St Edmundsbury Press, Bury St Edmunds, Suffolk

Contents

chapter   *page*

1   Journey around my Zaydeh   1
2   The Baby in the Family   8
3   The Ima   13
4   The Abah   21
5   God in my House   34
6   The war and blowing bubbles   38
7   The Zionist Dream   44
8   Physical Cowardice and Mental Courage   50
9   Sensual Pleasure and Moral Lessons in
      Atlantic City   55
10 Hello Happiness, Farewell Honesty   65
11 Foretaste of the World to Come   72
12 God in his House   78
13 It's his Money, let him spend it the
      way he wants   92
14 To Read Sforim or Books is the Question   99
15 Flirting with Sigmund Freud   107
16 'I vunt to see your Mudder, your Fadder
      or vun of your Parents'   115
17 My Beneficent Genie   129
18 In Spite of it All, Yes!   136
19 'Young Brichto, you must be in Love!'   141
20 Two Spies in the Camp   146

21 'Don't worry, Rabbi, one day you will
        get a congregation'   154
22 Praise the Lord I have been rejected!   161
23 The end and the beginning of the matter   164
    Epilogue   169
    Glossary of Hebrew and Yiddish words   170

I

Journey around my Zaydeh

Born in Philadelphia, Pa. USA, I still did not feel that I was an American. I was often told by my parents that, having been the only member of my family born in the USA, I could become the country's President, a privilege denied to my two brothers and one sister. They had to be satisfied with the *yichus*, spiritual merit, of being born in the holy city of Jerusalem. I was jealous of them. Their birth in the holiest city in the world was an accomplished fact. My becoming president had less chance than the Republican Party drafting Stalin for the job.

My entire family arrived in 1930, refugees from the world economic recession. It is an irony that, even in the great American depression, the USA was still considered the *goldena medina*, the golden country, and my family must have been among the first *yordim*, émigrés, of Sabras. How remarkable that I do not recall, as one would now, hearing expressions of guilt or excuses for their departure from the Holy Land!

I did not feel American because in my infancy I lived in a totally closed world. It was my family and the others. We were poor, situated in a poor neighbourhood in the inner city. By the time we moved in, most Jews had moved out to make room for the Negroes. It was considered racist in those days to refer to them as blacks or *schwartzes*.

I did not even have the benefit of a large Jewish family or community. My Zaydeh, grandfather, organised the emigration of his two daughters, his son and their families. He lived in West Philly where I was born. We moved to the north of the city away from him and my aunt, uncle and cousins. It was an hour's journey by bus and train, and it was a happy event when a visit to them was organized. My sense of aloneness was increased because I was the youngest in the family, my siblings being between seven and twelve years older than me.

I did not identify even with the poor Jews who lived in our neighbourhood because they, unlike us, were Americans on the way out of their poverty. They spoke English. They were shopkeepers or craftsmen. My parents spoke only Yiddish. They didn't even speak Hebrew because it was the holy tongue. I owe my name to their ignorance of English. Several days after my birth, the nurse registrar came round the wards to be told that I was to be named 'Shimshon' after my paternal great-grandfather. What was to be the English name? Research showed the translation to be Samson. When the registrar nurse heard this, she looked at me and protested on my behalf; 'You cannot name that poor child Samson'. 'What then?' my mother asked. And the answer was 'Sidney'.

So my parents spoke Yiddish, a strange language. Not only that, my father was in a business exclusive to Jews. He was a *shochet*: one who slaughtered chickens so that they were kosher. It is important for children to be proud of their parents. The Talmud said that God created mankind through one man, Adam, so that no person could say to another: 'My father was better than yours.' All the same, it was difficult for me to be proud of an occupation which was to kill defenceless chickens. He had the brains and knowledge to have become a rabbi but circumstances made him into a *shochet*. It was my uncle's luck, with the same background, to have become a rabbi who, according to my mother, would lie stretched out on the sofa most of the day reading newspapers, while my father was standing in a dust infested atmosphere, killing and plucking feathers off chickens. I remember how I watched in fascination as he sharpened his knife against a stone and then tested it over his fingernail to make certain that there was not the smallest nick in the blade, because that would have caused pain to the chicken and made it *trefe*, not kosher.

His work caused me embarrassment because my class-mates would ask me, 'What does your dad do?' Most did not know what a *shochet* was and I explained quite properly that he was a ritual slaughterer of chickens. This cir-cumlocutionary definition of *shochet* must have presented strange images in their mind. Did they imagine him dancing around chickens bound to a pole, chanting voodoo incanta-tions before slashing their throats? Perhaps one reason I was not beaten up more often for being Jewish was that this inspired respect and fear in them. It could be dangerous to mess around with a kid whose father was a 'ritual slaughterer'!

It is a matter of self-preservation to reinforce a sense of identity by taking pride in the source of one's being, in other words, one's parents. That for me meant taking pride in my parents' Jewishness. I remember walking on cold winter's nights with my hand in my father's coat pocket to keep it warm; feeling proud because, at the little *shul*, synagogue, to which we went, he was the most educated Jew. While he only led the prayers occasionally, he was officially the *Rav*, minister of the *shul*, and on this basis received a ten per cent clerical discount from Gimbels, a leading Phila-delphia department store, where he was registered as the Rev Solomon Brichta.

Later on, I took pride in the fact that he was the Hon Secretary of the Shochetim Union Local 493 of the Amer-ican Federation of Labour, the A F of L. Incredibly in the '40s and '50s Philadelphia could boast fifty poultry *shochetim*. I can testify to this because I folded the invitations for the Union meetings.

I was, of course, orthodox. On *erev Shabbat*, Sabbath eve, lights were switched on in the bathroom, the kitchen and living room, and would stay on throughout the Sab-bath while the rest of the house remained in darkness until three stars appeared in the sky on Saturday night. It was not permitted to switch electricity on or off on the holy day.

My Jewishness was my identity and the more I experienced it, the more secure I became. The degree of orthodoxy, however, was a source of some tension at home. My father would worry that my mother would be late in lighting the Sabbath candles. My mother reassured him that she would meet the deadline before sunset. I cannot quite remember the details but there always seemed to be discussions about the degrees of *kashrut*, dietary prohibitions, one should keep. My mother was more liberal. She boasted to me that of all the orthodox brides in Jerusalem, she was the only girl to put her foot down. Unlike the others, she would not have her head completely shaved before the wedding day, so as to make her less attractive to other men, and have her naked head covered by a kerchief. This was the custom in the orthodox neighbourhood before any marriage. She refused to be browbeaten by fanatical religiosity. Due to her iconoclastic spirit, being Jewish was not oppressive. If a friend carried my dime, I could even go to the movies on Sabbath and see the feature film plus the Superman or Batman serial.

We were un-American in the sense that we did not know about a life of vacations or Mother's Day and Valentine's Day cards. What I knew about was the buying of the yearly suit of clothes before *Rosh Hashanah*, the Jewish New Year, so that we could say a *Shehecheeyonu* – a blessing of thanksgiving, and, if it was a 'good year', a summer suit before Passover. What we knew about was special cakes called *Homentashen* on Purim, getting a smile and a pat on the back for being able to recite by heart on Passover Eve the 'Four Questions' in Hebrew and Yiddish at the *Seder*, the evening home service, and the pillow fights with the pillows on which we reclined during the ritual meal. What we as children knew about was the pride of extending the length of our fast on Yom Kippur. 'I fasted longer than you!' was how I competed with my cousins.

Then, there was the annual pilgrimage to the mansion

of the *Manistrichter rebbeh** for Rosh Hashanah and Yom Kippur, *the* Day of Atonement. My father was the *baal shaharit*, the leader of the morning prayers, the warm-up for the *hazan* or cantor who chanted the *mussaf*, an additional service which took place only on the Sabbath and festivals. The *Manistrichter* was a powerful figure, a giant of a man, well over six feet tall with enormous feet. When greeting me, he often lifted me in the air and I was frightened to be up so high. He had a well-groomed pitch-black beard. When he lifted me and gave me a cuddle, he would say, with the little command of English he had, 'Shimshon, you are a bad boy.' I defended myself, 'No, I am a good boy, you are a bad boy.' This amused him and became a ritual. I was the only one allowed to disagree with him. He was a tyrant with a fierce temper. Once when they ran out of wine at a meal with his Hasidim, in anger he slapped the face of his Hasidic benefactor who had provided the wine. What a *hutzpa* to skimp and embarrass the *rebbeh*!

These pilgrimages sadly ended when my mother, lacking in deference, told the *rebbetsin*, the wife of the *rebbeh*, to tell her husband that the portions of gefilte fish which she served were too miserly. She did so, and when the irate *rebbeh* heard the source of the criticism, our High Holyday visits ended. My father was then free to hire his services out to other congregations and sometimes we would walk miles on the High Holydays for this additional income.

If I had wanted to fantasize on how nice it would be to be a real American as well as a Jew, its impossibility was revealed to me as I made the long trek to synagogue on the Day of Atonement. My father was in his 'Sunday best' but with several anomalies to mar his image as a well-dressed man. Because Yom Kippur was a day when every Jew is

---

* *rebbeh* was the title given to Hasidic spiritual leaders and sometimes to those who taught the Talmud in a *yeshiva*, an Orthodox school of learning. A *rebbe*h unlike a rabbi did not need to be ordained as it was often an inherited post of a Hasidic dynasty.

commanded to afflict himself and to repent of all his sins, he not only had to refrain for twenty-four hours from eating and drinking and from sex, but he could not brush his teeth, wash, or wear leather shoes (which were considered a luxury and a sign of comfort). Thus my father in his best suit of clothing seemed rather weird to the onlooker as he had more than a five o'clock shadow (and this was before the time of fashionable designer stubble) and was sporting white sneakers. As we walked together hand in hand, my plimsolls seeking to keep up with his, and met the occasional gaze of passers-by, I realized that for the time being, at any rate, I could not be an American Jew, but would have to be proud of being a Jewish Jew.

The Zaydeh, my grandfather, made this pride possible. He was a scholar of the highest order. People would lift up their eyebrows in respect when they heard his name because of his rabbinic stature. He knew the Talmud on pin point, i.e. you could put a pin on any page in the Talmud and he could tell you the *sugya*, the discussion, on the same spot five pages forward or back. In my memory, he had a red beard, then a red-grey beard, then a grey beard. He had the habit of turning up the ends of his beard while he was in deep thought, and putting its ends between his lips. This usually happened when he interrupted his teaching of the Talmud because a new legal possibility occurred to him. He would knit his brows, play with his beard and we would wait entranced to see what the outcome would be. But he rarely told us. When he came out of his reverie, he would nod his head, smile and pick up where he left off. He smoked Prince Edward cigars and his students loved to watch him light up his cigar and then see the cellophane wrapper go up in flames.

He made me proud because he was recognised as the greatest Talmudist in Philadelphia. Frankel Teomim was a name to be reckoned with! He was the head of two Talmudical academies. I was proud to be his grandson. He taught me that Jews were superior because they studied.

Proper Jews didn't play ball or cards. They studied and came close to God because that was the way to enter God's mind. Somehow he made me believe that Jews who had the right to call themselves Jews studied Torah. The gentiles didn't. What they *did* do was to make the world go round but they could not sail through the sea of the Talmud. They knew how to make money and war and have fun in between but they did not know how to argue a proposition, to give a new interpretation to an old verse and to realise the significance of a *mitzvah,* commandment. They had their cars and vacations. We had our God and his Torah.

One story is sufficient to show the standards he put before me. At our table, he once asked: 'Shimshon, how many chickens *est a mensch*, does a man eat in his lifetime?' Before waiting for the answer, he made his own calculation. '*La mir zagen*, let us say, he eats chicken twice a week, *Freitag ba nacht oon Shabbos*, Friday night and Saturday, and each time a *fiertel*, a quarter. Half a chicken a week, 25 chickens a year. Say he lives to seventy or seventy-two, a person eats 1,850 chickens in his lifetime, maybe 2,000 because of holidays and *simhas,* happy events. A man eats maybe 2,000 chickens! I ask you what right has he to do so? I tell you what right he has! A human being is a superior life. He can think, he can study, he can talk to God, he can do *mitzvot*. When he eats a chicken he raises it to a higher *madrega*, level, but if he doesn't do all these things; if he only eats, drinks and fornicates, he is just like an animal, and has no right to eat a chicken. *Du fashtayst Shimshon?* You understand?' I understood his syllogism. People of the intellect were superior. Jews were of the higher intellect, and ergo Jews, including me, were superior. Jewish elitism? Maybe. But I am grateful to him for *it* was the key to my emotional survival.

2

The Baby in the Family

I was the baby in my family. It was not until I was older that I realised that this was a title and a condition from which there was no escaping. Were I to live to ninety, I would still be the baby in my family. Being the baby, therefore, is an ageless category, causing problems as well as bestowing privileges. It suggests being particularly loved, even if you are not, and spoilt, even if you are not.

One thing is for certain, in my child's world: it gave me a distinction. I became special to myself because, 'Sidney is the baby in the family'. The repetition of that descriptive phrase gives one an identity, and for a child an identity of any nature is very important. I am sure it has been written before that there exists a paradox for the growing child. He is told to stop acting like a child when that is after all what he is. And when he seeks to assert his independence, he is reprimanded for lack of respect to parents and adults in general: 'You are still a child, and how dare you behave in such a way?' In such a confusing world set by adults, in which children grope for some clarification of their existence, *any* identity helps. Are there not children who remain brats because, were they to lose that description, they would lose the identifying characteristics by which they had come to know themselves. Who can tell? Perhaps some people remain shy all their lives because as infants they were described in this way and feel obliged forever to fit that mould?

What did my identity as the baby mean for me? Well, it meant that I had stolen affection from my brother and, as there was not much affection going around in my family, that was quite a serious crime. 'Poor little fellow, he was so upset when we brought Sidney home.' I was constantly told how his emotional problems began because I had dispossessed him as the baby, putting him into the no-man's-land of middle brother. And this heavy burden was placed upon me in spite of the fact that I was told that I was an unwanted 'accident'. My mother was thirty-six and poor with three children and she had enough *tsoros*, troubles, without me. She went to the doctor, had hot baths, drank tonic water: 'It had helped as much as applying leeches to a corpse!' So not only did I not ask to be born, but no one else wanted me to be born, and yet, strange as it may appear, my earliest emotional recollection is not of being rejected but of guilt for taking the babyship from my brother. I had stolen his identity.

Ironically, so great is the instinct of self-preservation, abetted by the fact that my accidental birth was mentioned to me without embarrassment, that I *even* became proud of it. I had had to fight for my existence. 'Hey, you know what? I am an accident, how about you?' In my world, there were two categories, the babies and the non-babies, the accidents and the non-accidents. My poor brother, he was neither and it was my fault. I grew up to be afraid of him, and not because he was anything but nice to me. He was a very good-natured fellow. Only once did I have cause to hate him. When I was seven years old, the U.S. Mint produced the 1943 silver-looking pennies and I was saving them in an empty Watermans ink bottle. When the bottle was almost full, he took them to buy comics. I felt like Silas Marner when he could not find his gold.

My fear of him, however, was due to projection. If he had deprived me of my identity, as I had deprived him of his, I would have killed him. It was an unconscious fear, but by the time I was approaching nine, and he was going through adolescence, I would go to sleep with trepidation in the room we shared, lest he stab me during the night. I made sure that there were no scissors lying about, just in case he had an uncontrollable urge to get even with me.

My parents tell a story. It seems that one day while I was

lying in my pram, he sat on the handlebar. The pram flipped and I flew out and hit my head against the radiator! Unlike in England, even poor families had hot water radiators in the 1930s. I had forgotten the story until once, when rubbing the back of head, I felt a very flat surface on an otherwise round globe. That must have been where I made contact with the radiator. Perhaps, that is why I am not good at maths and languages. The grey matter in those areas of competency had been crushed!

In Biblical tales, as well as in Greek mythology, we see the most basic human experiences writ large in the lives of individual heroes and demi-gods. There are many instances of the baby in the family becoming the favourite. Isaac chosen over Ishmael by Sarah, Jacob over Esau by Rebecca, Joseph over his brothers by Jacob. True, Benjamin was younger than Joseph but in a family of twelve sons, don't call me a liar for being one out! Samuel, the Seer, ignored the seniority of his seven elder brothers when choosing David to be king of Israel.

I could not, however, find a paradigm for the rejected middle brother until I recalled the three sons of Noah who survived the flood with their father and thus became the ancestors for all mankind. They were, in age order, Shem, Ham and Japhet. Shem is the ancestor of the Semites, from whom the Hebrews are descended. Japhet is the father of Yavan, the ancestor of the Greeks. Matthew Arnold in his essay on Hebraism and Hellenism highlighted the polarities of Jewish morality and Greek aesthetics. The book of Genesis foretells the reconciliation of the two great forces in civilised life by saying that Shem will dwell in the tents of Japhet.

But what of the middle brother, Ham? He is the ancestor of the Canaanites, who are to be conquered by the Hebrews, as well as of the Egyptians and the tribes of Africa. Ham is cursed by Noah for the offence of gloating over the latter's nakedness when he became drunk after his invention of wine. His curse is that he is to be a slave to his brothers.

Thus even the Bible rationalises the unhappy situation of the middle brother, and gives it primordial significance. This did not assuage my guilt for dispossessing my brother of his position as the baby. Because of it, I never resented the showering of presents on him as my father sought to compensate him for his emotional sufferings. These were my guilt offerings as well, and I remember my pleasure when he received his first car, a 1939 Oldsmobile, purchased in 1949 for $350.

Like all babies, I had to assert myself to get attention, particularly as there was a large age difference between me and all the members of my family. That meant talking a lot and loudly and very quickly, lest I wasn't given the chance to finish the sentence. I recall smiling as I remember asking my own baby, also the youngest of four children, 'Must you talk all the time? Do you have to have the last word? We do not need a running commentary on all your activities. You know it is possible to exist without speaking!' My smile turned into repressed laughter as I remembered being offered a nickel by my older brother if I could keep quiet for five minutes and my inability to meet the challenge. Beyond the achievement of an identity, I do not recall any privileges of being the baby. I received no more affection, nor was I given a favoured position. Like King Lear I had the title, the position without the power.

The one distinction was that on the first two nights of Passover, at the *Seder* (which is the home religious service when families relive the story of the Exodus from Egypt) I would begin the proceedings by asking the formulaic four questions after which the narrative unfolds. For several weeks before the *Seder*, I memorised the Hebrew Questions and their translation into Yiddish. In sing-song I would begin, 'Father, I wish to ask you four questions.' Once I had bumbled these questions out in two strange languages, my father would nod and, reclining on his chairs joined together like a chaise longue, would say in Yiddish: 'Now let us repeat the questions', as if to say, that what I had done was not sufficient to fulfil the ritual. So this was my only moment of organised glory throughout the year. All other recognition and fame had to be fought for on equal terms with the rest of the world. Also, for what it is worth, on Saturday night to mark the end of the Sabbath, blessings were said over wine, a lit multi-wicked candle and spices. As the baby, I would hold the candle and was told that as high as I held it, so tall would be the woman I married. While getting hot wax on my hands was slightly painful, I still welcomed the attention but could not imagine that 'babies' ever got married.

What was most strange was the feeling that I have had throughout my life of not quite growing up, of having to assert and prove myself, of feeling younger than people younger than myself, a whole complex of feelings of insecurity and arrogance which may be the baggage of the baby of the family. Until middle age, I often had the feeling that I was bluffing the world, that I would be found out for the sham that I was, and it was a revolutionary moment in my life, when the truth became an emotional reality for me. I was no longer faking it. My achievements were real, my sentiments sincere, and I was a person like others. If it were possible, I had at last transcended being the baby of the family.

3

The Ima

The source of my being is my mother, the Ima, the derivative
of the Hebrew word *Aim*, meaning mother. At her door I lay
most of my emotional problems, but also there I must lay my
capacity for overcoming them. I loved her dearly, as I am
sure she loved me, but unfortunately for her she was not
able to express this love except in the most limited and
restricted fashion. My readers may weep for me and wish to
give me a compensatory cuddle, when I tell them of my
experiences. But let them think as do I of the children who
are beaten by parents and strangers, whose bellies protrude
because of lack of nourishment, whose eyes can hardly open
because of insect bites, and my situation will appear in
proper perspective.

Still, the fact that children were not eating in India, as my
mother told me, and yours may have told you, did not
improve my appetite. So too, the far worse physical and emotional deprivation of other children did not diminish my own
confusion. I call it this because the solicitous attention she
gave me, the efforts she made on my behalf and the pride she
took in me were in diametric contradiction to the fact that
she never kissed or embraced me. I do not recall the parental
smile of love, which gives radiance to a child's life, the aware-
ness that mum or dad has sneaked into your bedroom to
make sure that you are all right, the feel of the blanket
being raised over you to keep you warm. My only memory of
bodily contact with her was after the bi-weekly bath at the
age of four or five, when she would carry me piggyback to my
bed. I felt then the absorption of spiritual warmth which I
missed the rest of the week. I can see in my mind's eye and

feel as though it were yesterday, the picture of the little boy, aged six, in the kitchen, looking at his mother's face with its sharp features, loving it even though it was sad, because it was his mother's, and this made it beautiful, and wanting to go up to kiss her and not knowing how. The moment was so intense that the image is frozen in time. She looked angelic, her face seemed to be yearning to be touched and kissed. I wanted to go up to her and just touch it, but how could I? How would I indicate my desire? She was beyond my reach physically as well as emotionally. I could not come upon her by surprise. Small as she was, she was still too tall for me. Would I approach and say, 'Ima, I want to kiss you, please bend down and let me kiss you?' But what if she had said, 'What foolery, what do you want?' So I could not and did not.

A later event made me feel I had been wise not to take the risk. My heart was broken when she did not have the generosity of spirit to receive a box of chocolates in the shape of a red heart which my middle brother had given her on Valentines Day, and for which he had saved. 'How much did it cost?' she asked and 'How could you have spent so much money on a box of chocolates?' was the thanks he had for stretching out to her. If it broke my heart, what did it do to him?

She was aware that she did not display affection. She defended herself by poking sarcastic fun at her sister for her treatment of my cousins, 'She kisses and she smacks, I neither kiss nor smack'. How often did I want to tell her how much I would have preferred being smacked if that meant also being kissed? I would have welcomed physical expressions of anger rather than the long hurt look of disappointment which would make me cry in shame. In order to defend her failure, she had gone overboard. She had rationalised it into a virtue. She was not a sentimentalist!

Yet, she was an irredeemable romantic. She was the woman who had a song in her heart, but could not sing, for she had no voice, no ear, and did not even know the notes.

The Ima lost her own Ima when she was a babe in arms. Her father, the Zaydeh, was an abstracted intellectual, who had never known anything but scholarship and study since a child. He must have been the Jewish equivalent to Samuel Butler, who recounts memorising Greek declensions at the age of three. From my knowledge of him, he had sublimated all his emotions into the love of Torah and so could not even give normal paternal affection even less be a mother substitute. The Ima told me that she did not walk until she was four. Was this her protest at taking the steps towards independence without a mother to nurse her along?

Being a woman in a male-dominated society, she had no schooling, no challenge to test her wits in the intricacies of Talmudic disputes, no opportunity for winning recognition in the mastery of Jewish texts. Without love, without motivation for achievements, and without natural beauty, what had she left but fantasy, none of which was ever capable of fulfilment? Religiously, she read the serial romances in the Yiddish *Forwards* and this won the contempt of my father. The men of that scholarly Jewish world never read a novel. A novel was referred to as a *roman*, a romance, something for young girls and old women to read. My father never could understand my own passion for novels, nor could he believe that it was the way to culture. How could story-telling be anything but an inferior use of time when there was God's word to study? There was no room for my mother in this world, so she had to create her own. She did. A sharp intellect without a function, a heart without love, all she could do was to divide her life between the duty of being a good mother and wife and the romances of forsaken wives, betrayed lovers, and ungrateful children. In between these two worlds was the gossip which sought to make the lives of family and friends more exciting than they were. The exchanges of mutual disappointment, disapproval and shock at the behaviour of intimates became the meat of the starved imagination of poor Jewish housewives, when it was not feeding on the tragedies unfolding in the Yiddish journals.

For lack of exercise and purpose, the Ima's intellect was turned to the logic of skimping and saving and obtaining value for money, of prudently charting our slow ascent into the world of material pleasures. In the development of her shrewdness she reminded me of the peasant women of Maupassant and the middle-class women of Balzac. Once she felt that enough money had been saved, the time had come to buy a modest house, then the time to buy the living room furniture, then the dining table and chairs, then carpets and so on. Every purchase was carefully considered. Occasionally there would be an unexpected opportunity: a service of German silver for sale second-hand; a beautiful elmwood bedroom set bought from a neighbour moving or selling up. She would jump at the chance to make money, as when she helped an estate agent sell a house to an acquaintance. I remember my tiny, Ima slightly bent over, going quickly down the street to collect her $50 commission for the sale, and her pride when she returned home with the money in her purse.

She only went to retail shops when there were sales. On all other occasions, she went to wholesalers or jobbers. I remember to my horror one day, when choosing a tie in the sale, she noticed that the one she had selected was not discounted as much as another in the same rack. She immediately exchanged the price tags. 'Ima, you can't do that,' I protested in dismay. 'Sidney, don't be a fool. What difference does it make, they are the same ties. It was a mistake by the shopkeeper. I slunk away from the cash register as she made her purchase. The effect this had on my moral development, I can only surmise.

She did not believe in luxuries or fripperies but we had the necessities. We had proper clothes and they were always clean. When I complained that other children had birthday celebrations and presents, my persuasive powers resulted in being presented one birthday with a pair of socks in a brown paper bag. I never had a birthday card or party. The reason I had to remind my family of my birthday was that I had two of them. From my father's point of view, I was born on the 2nd day of the Hebrew month of Av. Because I was an American, my birthday was on the 21st of July. These dates never or rarely coincided because they were based on two different calendars, the Solar and Lunar. The consequence of having two birthdays was not having even one.

My mother was very dutiful. It was she who went to open days at school. It was she who determined my education. I was embarrassed when I compared my mother to others. They were young, sprightly and American. The Ima looked ancient, bent over and a refugee. She did not give me pride, and my shame filled me with guilt.

I do not recall any exchanges of affection between the Ima and the Abah, though I do recall some laughter in bed between them when I was still sleeping in a cot in their bedroom. My father revealed a streak of sadism in his relationship to the Ima. Was that because his own need for affection was thwarted? Before giving in to any demand for money for a purchase, he would argue and argue and it was only when she broke down in tears that he gave in. This may have been the only way he knew of getting an emotional reaction from her or a form of vengeance for not getting it, or both.

With all her disadvantages, the key to the Ima's survival was her determination and obstinacy. She had to believe in herself, and she did. What she did was always right. That was her security, and she did not give a fig for the rest of the world. As an adolescent, I questioned her on the strangeness of the fact that she was always right. She responded in a plea for sympathy, 'I wish I was wrong sometimes. Can I help it if I am always right!'

I never felt rejected by her because it was not personal for she had rejected the world. When I was older, I felt very sorry for her when she spoke to me about herself. Sitting on the beach in Atlantic City with her, on one of our rare vacations, she told me that love disappears in marriage and that the bond between a mother and child was greater than that between husband and wife, because they were ties of blood. I was too embarrassed to argue with her but I did not believe that this had to be the case.

She was houseproud. The house was her fortress against the world and it had to be ready for battle at all times. That meant no dust on surfaces, no creases in the sofa, no dishes left overnight. We protested that she scooped up the plate before you had eaten the meal and beat out the depression in the pillow the moment you arose from the sofa. This was a cause for laughter in the family which made her feel sad and misunderstood.

Her sense of security was increased by working to schedule. While there were no weekly postings of menus, there was meat on Monday and Wednesday and dairy foods on Tuesdays and Thursdays. The weekend was dominated by the Sabbath when it was chicken soup, gefilta fish and chicken both for Friday supper and Saturday lunch. Saturday night was herring or some sort of snack delicatessen food. I cannot remember Sunday because memories of food for that day coalesce with my making myself corn beef or pastrami rolls which I ate while watching the Philadelphia baseball teams, the Phillies or the 'A's playing their Sunday double-header on television.

Having been rejected in infancy by the loss of her mother, and without any compensation for this loss, Ima could not be giving. But this did not prevent her from expecting from others the expressions of affection and concern which she subconsciously was not able to accept. She was a pathetic figure. My father and my siblings poked fun at her for her foibles and her seriousness, for she had little humour. To smile and to laugh would suggest that the world and life were not unrelieved misery and this was a spiritual compromise she was not prepared to make. She must have smiled and laughed on occasions. I seem to recall that those were moments when she laughed at others, not herself. There was really no fun in her life. She only attended a few films, for the English was too difficult for her to understand. Her only

social entertainment was the *Simha*, the engagement party,
wedding or Bar Mitzvah celebration.

Life was duty. Even the Sabbath and Festivals gave her no
joy. True, she was compelled to rest for part of these Holy
Days because she was not allowed to wash and clean. She
would moan, however, at the work involved in the preparation for the Festivals. It was a man's world, and the Jewish
holidays were for men and not for her. The family *Seder* was
joyous for everyone but her, and one could sympathise with
her. She did all the work with no help from my father. He
felt no guilt in this matter. He worked hard throughout the
week. Was it not right for him at least to take pleasure in
doing God's commandments? Was he called upon to set the
tables and help with the food? Surely this was the role of
women. What else had they to do? He would comfortably
recline at the *Seder*, as his father had done, reading the
Haggadah, the Passover Service, and she would sit there
grim-faced waiting for the moment when we would have
to rise to serve the many course meal. Judaism was no fun.
She felt it blatantly unfair, and who today would not agree
with her?

But we at that time were not of a mind to give her sympathy. Often guilt would stir us into some activity on her
behalf but, as there could be no expression of affection, the
only emotional avenue open was conflict. This led to arguments on any and every possible issue. She would weep as
she felt misunderstood by all. Only occasionally did one of
the family take her side, the way one supports the underdog,
regardless of the rights and wrongs of the situation. As she
grew older, she felt increasingly unappreciated and rejected.
She began to protect herself from hurt by closing herself off
from any complicated relationships which caused pain. My
father left their flat and became a boarder with a niece and
her family. Slowly but surely, she cut herself off from the life
she could not control, which gave her so little and to which
she could give nothing in return. As long as I can remember,
she complained of a 'nervous' stomach. I never knew what

that meant but I gathered that, by giving it that name, she was telling us that it was incurable. She died aged sixty-nine, of pneumonia, which my older brother told me was the consequence of emphysema, a disease of the lungs which makes breathing painfully difficult. Based on my visit to her before her death, I think it was the death of the life force in her. She had given up.

To understand is to forgive and I have forgiven her for depriving me of the emotional nourishment, which made me less of a person because of this. But I find it difficult to forgive myself for not understanding earlier and for not trying to repay her for what she *did* do for me. She cared for me! She defended me and supported my efforts and sought to fulfil whatever desires I was able to formulate for myself! She deserved better from me, as she deserved better from the world, but can that not be said of most decent, ordinary, good people, amongst whom I would include the Ima.

4

The Abah

I was thrilled! The best report card I had ever received. Seven As and a B+. I showed it first to the Ima because the Abah was, reciting his afternoon prayers. '*Zayer gut*', she said, after I read it to her. 'Show it to the Abah.' I handed it to him. As he was in the midst of prayer, he couldn't talk, but by that weird combination of a sense of familiarity with God and the belief that formal prayer was primarily an exercise of Jewish discipline, he had no qualms at looking at the report while continuing to mutter his prayers by rote. He, of course, knew all the daily prayers by heart. So would you if you had said them as often as he had: three times a day, seven days a week, fifty-two weeks a year and for fifty years.

He looked at the report, lifted his face up to me, pointed at the B+ and gave me a disapproving and quizzical look. To this very day, I do not know whether he was joking or serious. What amazes me now is my recollection of my response. I was not crestfallen, nor was I upset. That was the Abah. Had I remonstrated with him for his lack of praise and recognition, he would have said, 'That's a compliment. It shows what I expect from you.' So, what was the use?

Much later, I read that mothers give unconditional love but that fathers require that their love be earned through the fulfilment of expectations. An interesting theory: maternal love is the basis of security, paternal love is the motivating force for achievement. This neat polarity can be expanded into the States of 'Being' and 'Becoming'. A child who has enjoyed great effusions of maternal love will never need to justify his right to be. He who has had little of such love but a demanding father will feel that living must be justified by achieving objectives. Philosophically, George Santayana's dualism of Piety and Idealism fits in nicely with this theory. Love and loyalty to the past and its traditions is defined as Piety; the need to move forward to break with tradition and to improve on the past is the basis of Idealism: the expectations of a God who is *avinu malkaynu*, our father as well as our king.

The Abah, however, *never* let me know that he had any expectations of me. My Jewish talmudic background provided me with a series of assumptions. Being a descendant of *talmiday hahamim**, I was going to be bright, a good student and successful in whatever I decided to do. If these assumptions were realised, that was only to be expected: if not, then I became a problem. My father, therefore, provided me with no guidelines and made no demands. There was neither praise nor reproach, neither advice nor admonition. I did not blame him then for his passiveness. A child only judges by the standards set for him by his parents. I do not blame him now, because I know that he was a victim of his own upbringing. He had lived all his life in a closed society and the same assumptions were made about him as were made about me.

Consider that my great-grandfather Shimshon Peterfreund, after whom I am named, left his home in Jerusalem in the late 1870s to visit the head of the *yeshiva* in Nitra, Czechoslovakia. After the normal salutations and description of how it fared in the Holy Land, he came to the reason for his journey. He wanted a husband for his daughter, Channa, and knowing of the reputation of the *yeshiva*, he had come to request one of its best young lads, to go up to the Holy Land where, after marrying Channa, he could continue his studies supported by his father-in-law.

---

* Literally, 'disciples of the wise'. A class system that developed in Jewish culture between the learned and the ignorant. This was unlike the distinction between the educated and the uneducated because it had to do with those who had the facilities to study the Talmud and learn exactly the nature and demands of the Jewish Law

The *Rosh yeshiva*, the Principal, considered the request which he had anticipated, for this was one of many such visitors who had come with this objectives. He recommended Shmuel Brichta, his best student. His antecedents and scholarship, were discussed, and it was decided to seek his agreement. The *Rosh yeshiva* would not be happy to lose such a student, but he could not deprive the lad the opportunity to settle in Palestine, no matter how much he would miss him. The young man agreed and after the necessary discussion with the *machtonim*, his future in-laws, he set out with my great-grandfather, not in the style of Rebecca accompanying Eliezer to meet her future husband, Isaac, the son of the patriarch Abraham, but with the same principle in mind, to maintain the best Jewish eugenics, the marriage of scholarship and piety combined with wealth or beauty. Shmuel married Channa, continued his studies, had an appropriate number of children. The time came when my grandfather Shmuel Brichta, took on gainful employment as a general secretary to an organisation responsible for dispensing welfare funds from abroad to local Jews in need.

My father, who was born in 1902, was raised to a life of study. He ate, he studied and he slept. He never played ball. That was considered an amusement akin to playing cards, behaviour which one would only expect from *am haratzim*, literally, people of the land, peasants, but used metaphorically to encompass all who eschewed the study of the sacred books. They were to live their lives with no other purpose than enjoying themselves, or in the case of the kibbutzniks, creating a socialist society in which all would have equal opportunity for pleasure. While there was some admiration for the idealism of the kibbutzniks it was no substitute for the ennoblement that came from the study of the Torah. When I expressed surprise to my father that he played the traditional games of *dreidel*, a gambling top and *quitlach*, a form of blackjack, only on the one day of Purim when gambling was approved; and that he never as a child or young man took a break from his studies to play at any other time, he said to me: 'Shimshon, you cannot understand the excitement of studying which was ours.' I could, but what did surprise me was how the mores which he and his fellow students had imbibed from birth had conditioned them to be contemptuous of any style of life different from their own. The fact is that they all lived in a talmudic ghetto, all shared the same values, where one worked because of necessity but would have preferred to devote all one's time to study, and where a person who was able to study and maintain a family at someone else's expense was considered no more a parasite than a university fellow on a research grant.

This meant that no demands were made on my father by his father. It was the culture inbred over generations for the men to study and for the women to look after them and the children they sired. What the Abah forgot was that, in coming to America, the change in environment required for him a change in attitude and practice. He was, however, unprepared or unable to treat me differently than he was treated. All continued it was assumed, to be as it had been in the past. He did not even tell me about his own upbringing, and so I did not know until much later what these assumptions were. Indeed, I had always thought that it was just the Zaydeh, who had had such rigorous upbringing. It was not until he was eighty-six years old that the Abah told me, and only under my questioning, that he too had never thought of enjoying life in any other way than through the observance of *mitzvot* and the study of Torah.

He never played with me and I never expected him to. He never taught me and I never expected him to. Curiously, he was still surprised by my ignorance on any Jewish subject and reproached me for it. He felt that I should have known it either through inheritance of acquired characteristics or osmosis. So natural in me was respect for my father, that I felt guilty for my ignorance rather than the anger, at not being taught, to which I would have been entitled. Whatever he had was given to him by his surroundings, and when he came to America he had not learnt how to pass the essence of this all-embracing environment on to his children.

Significantly, his marriage to my mother had not been arranged. The Zaydeh, my mother's father, in the year of their courtship and marriage, in 1922, was in the U.S. He had gone to the States to become a head of *Yeshiva Aytz Chayeem*, Tree of Life, in New York City. He had done this for several years, until circumstances led him to become a successful insurance salesman. When my parents married, he sent them a present of $200, with which my father eventually opened a grocery store. But it went bankrupt during the Great Depression. The Abah, as a matter of respect, consulted the head of his Talmudical Academy about his proposed marriage to Rivka Frankel-Thomim. The *Rosh yeshiva* approved of the match because of her father's scholarship, but he expressed one reservation, that she might induce my father to leave for the U.S. My father told me this only recently. He smiled and said:

'He was right'.
'Are you sorry you came to America?'
'Yes'.
'Why?'
'Because I would rather my children had remained *gitten yiddin* and *yiray shamayim*, good Jews and God fearing'.
'Why did you come then?'
'Your Ima wanted me to make a living.'

The Abah must have felt that the move from Jerusalem to Philadelphia would have irreversible consequences on the nature of his children's Jewishness, but he was still unable to make the effort required to keep us on the straight and narrow path. Was it lack of training? Was it laziness, or was it despair of his inability to fight the forces of a land in which he was a stranger. Born in the old city of Jerusalem, totally at home with himself as a Jewish Jew, the shock of his transplantation into foreign soil must have been traumatic. For example, in the then Palestine, no self-respecting Orthodox Jew would be without a *sukkah*, an external booth built in gardens or on roofs on which to celebrate the festival of Tabernacles. For the war years 1939-45, constrained by our poverty, we lived in a second-floor flat, and my father had no *Sukkah* in which to eat his meals during the festival. He was devastated by this change in circumstances. Material poverty was insignificant to him. He had never known riches or physical comfort, but ritual and spiritual deprivation was something to which he had not been accustomed.

At the end of the war our circumstances changed. My father had saved enough to put down a deposit and afford a mortgage on a house. We moved to Logan, a nice suburb. It was within our means because wealthier Jews were beginning to move out of Logan to Oak Lane and Olney. But the streets were still wide and there were trees in front of each house. They were attached houses with covered front porches. The backyards were postage stamp size but big enough for a *sukkah*. For my father this was probably the move's greatest benefit. Of all the festivals he was happiest during that of Tabernacles, because he had achieved the ritual riches of being able to eat in a temporary shack in his garden. For me the benefit was sharing a twin bedded room with my brother, instead of sleeping in a double bed with my sister. Before we moved to a house my middle brother slept on a sofa bed in the living room. My older brother had already gone to Yeshiva University, ostensibly to become a rabbi, but in truth to avoid military draft.

The Abah, like my mother, did not show physical affection. Because he had not played, he did not play with his children. Indeed toys were considered a waste of money. How I came to have them, I do not remember, but my only two toys were a tiny model milk-wagon with play bottles and an Abraham Lincoln log cabin. I spent hours filling and unfilling the wagon and building and demolishing that log cabin. They gave me so much pleasure, that I would be overjoyed were I ever to be reunited with these sole reminders of myself at play. My father's smile and good sense of humour did however give me a sense of warmth. He was easy going and non-confrontational. I enjoyed being with him, because he was popular with all his colleagues. But, as a child, it was I who had to stretch out my hand to clasp his when we walked together.

One incident will give you some idea of the nature of our relationship. I was fifteen and the surgeon had agreed that I was sufficiently strong to have an operation on my hernia. Had he been approached several years earlier, he would have probably given the same answer then and saved me years of anguish and embarrassment. Into Mt Sinai I went. Confidently I was wheeled into the operating theatre, believing that the anaesthetic would kill all pain. One of my great complaints against the members of my family is that they tell me nothing until it is too late. No one told me of the pain after the operation, the sickness caused by the anaesthetic, the wind in the stomach which would not go away and the pain caused by every movement, including laughter. I was angry, 'why was I so misled?' Stoical pride made me hide it, but when I was told that the new hospital regimen was that you had to walk the day after the operation. I protested: I couldn't do it. The nurses did not make me, but when I had to relieve myself, they made me walk to the toilets. My father was there and accompanied me the 50 yards and I moaned that my insides were falling out. Finally I made it and sat down on the toilet seat. My Abah cannot tolerate pain, the pain of others as well as his own. He appeared to be suffering more than me during that trek to the toilet. He was suffering still when I heard him say from the front of the cubicle opening, 'Sidney, would you like a cigarette?' 'No, thank you Abah'. I didn't smoke and he knew it. But I was touched by this sign of affection and comeraderie. He felt that I was suffering like a man and, therefore, deserved a cigarette. Sadly, he also must have felt that was all he could offer me.

After I rejected orthodoxy at the age of fifteen and left home for good at eighteen, the spiritual separation between us became more obvious to me reinforced as it was by physical distance. I felt that I had let him down, because he could only interpret my rejection of orthodoxy as a personal slight on him and his values. He must have felt guilt too, a sense of failure at his inadequacy; but this, true to form, he could not share with me.

I interpreted one event as a muted expression of his anger and frustration. My brother Chanan, while a Chaplain in Korea, had sent me a charming set of Hindu gods. There must have been about nine of them in alabaster or hardened plastic, each about 1½ inches tall and less than an inch wide. With the set came a black painted two-tiered stand. Lovingly, I would arrange these statues on the stand, changing their position every once in a while for the sheer pleasure of holding them in my hands, but with the excuse that I could make them appear more impressive in a different order. One afternoon, I came into my room and saw that the gods had been scattered helter-skelter on my desktop. What had happened? We had no cat or dog, which could have been responsible. Good orthodox Jews in those days thought that pets were *goyish*. The cleaning woman who came in one day a week would have put them back had she decided to dust them. My mother, as you know by now, hated disorder, so she could not have been the culprit.

It could have only been my father! What feelings must have welled up in him to make him act like our Patriarch Abraham who declared his belief in One God by smashing his father's idols? Was this the story in reverse: an angry father demolishing the idols sent to me by my older brother, in whose footsteps he feared I was about to follow; symbolically attacking the new gods of the West (while in actuality attacking the old gods of the East) which were taking me away from him and the God he worshipped? He never said that he did it and I never asked him. The manner of this unresolved confrontation gives a powerful pointer to the lack of communication between father and son.

It was his Prostate Operation at Shaare Tzedek (Gate of

Righteousness) Hospital in Jerusalem on the night following the conclusion of Yom Kippur which enabled me to settle accounts for that cigarette he offered me and for so much more he didn't. He had returned to Jerusalem following his retirement in 1963, where he had purchased a small flat two years previously. My older brother Chanan had telephoned from Cincinnati to say that the Abah was undergoing surgery, and one of us should be there, since he was an old man with no one to look after him. I, in London, was much closer to Israel and I should be the one to go. I took this as a command and following the Day of Atonement Service, having broken the fast, my bags already packed the day before, my wife drove me to Heathrow for the late night El Al flight. At 2:30 am, I negotiated a taxi and was driven to the hospital with a recklessness which convinced me that I was heading in the right direction, even were my father not there. My hands shaking, I gave the driver three five pound notes, thanked him for saving my life from his own driving, for which courtesy, he allowed me, lugging my case, to find the main entrance and the porter who would tell me where to find the Abah.

My self appreciation for performing the double *mitzvah* of *kibud av*, respect for one's father and *bikur cholim*, visiting the ill, shot up enormously as I entered my father's twelve bedded ward. It looked like a World War I hospital ward which one imagines were made purposely decrepit to punish those who achieved survival by the strategies of getting a limb blown off. I had no trouble finding him. I could recognise the Brichto *krechs*, moan, anywhere. I dropped my bag and darted to his side. 'Abah', I said. He turned to me in gratitude and in disbelief turning into belief, said, 'Shimshon, *du bist du?*' 'Yes Abah, I am here'. '*B'vakasha, m'at mayim*, please a little water'. In Israel, he primarily spoke Hebrew, not Yiddish, as an act of patriotism and a sign of his own theological progress, since the days when spoken Hebrew was not permitted during his childhood because it was a holy tongue and not be used for profane purposes. The rebirth of modern Hebrew must be considered one of the great Jewish triumphs, not only because it was the revival of a dead language, but because even the ultra-orthodox were prepared to concede this victory to those secular Jews who had given them back their sovereignty, in spite of the fact that they would have preferred to have received it from a Jewish Messiah, garbed in a *shtreimel*, fur-trimmed hat, long morning coat and trailing *payos*, side locks behind his ears.

That night I ministered to my father's needs. I found a big storage chest near him on which with my coat as my pillow, I was able to sleep for an hour or so while he slumbered fitfully. He was suffering from pain, shock and disorientation. I brought him water, carried his complaints to the night nurse, brought back to him her reassurance. Occasionally she would accompany me, and say in Yiddish, '*Reb Shloime, alles vet zein gut*, all will be well'. She spoke in Yiddish because she was not aware that he had been born in Jerusalem and knew Hebrew, but thought that he was one of those thousands of Eastern Europeans, who had settled in America, had grown prosperous there and had come to live their last years in Jerusalem to die on holy ground. I remember his weak smile of acknowledgment when the nurse said how wonderful it was that his son had come all the way from England, left his family and work to be with him. For the first time in my life, I felt that my father was proud of me.

And so it went. For three nights I stayed at his bedside, sleeping in his flat during the afternoon when he had other visitors and several nurses to meet his needs. He slowly improved and his face beamed as he introduced me to visitors, 'This is my son, Shimshon, my youngest who lives in England.' The response was invariably, *Sehr shane*, very fine, or in Hebrew, *Yofi*, wonderful. That he should come from England! Everyone should have such a son! It seemed to me that more than my ministrations, what helped his recovery was basking in the recognition by his peers that he had a devoted son, which to some extent made amends for my heresy.

My father was in hospital during the festival of Tabernacles. I witnessed the extraordinary sight of old men, with ailing kidneys, livers and bladders, comparing the beauty of their citrons* with those of fellow patients. They performed the rite by shaking the *lulav*, palm branch, (embellished with myrtle and weeping willows) and the *etrog*, citron to east, west, north and south, earthwards and to the sky to declare God's omnipresence and sovereignty. My experience of seeing these men queuing up to enter the tiny 3 by 2 foot *sukkah* on the fire escape landing to shake what appeared to me as phallic symbols will never leave me. In addition to the *lulav* and *etrog* which they carried, some also dragged along bottles filling up with their bile. Pain and suffering was set aside as these old Jews hallowed their lives by obeying God's commandments.

For some reason, I had felt it appropriate to read for the third time Dostoevsky's *The Brothers Karamazov* during this journey to my Abah. I had begun reading on the plane and continued it in hospital, while my father rested, and in his flat before going to bed. I finished it the evening before I returned home, which was some six days after my arrival.

The Brothers Karamazov is for me the greatest novel ever written, touching the major existential themes of life. Once again I found myself in a world, full of hidden meanings and human relationships with all their love and violence. One of the novel's great themes is that, if God is dead, all is permitted. Allied to this theme is the idea that every son wishes for the death of his father for only then can he feel free to be himself and to forge his own destiny. As I read, I could only conclude that Dostoevsky was the product of an absolutist and tyrannical system. He did not know the God of the Jews who had developed from the stern judge to the loving father. Nor did Dostoevsky have a father like mine, who because of his background had always remained the child of his

---

* A citrus fruit resembling a lemon with an attached stem. Should the stem break off it becomes unfit for ritual use

environment, saddened when life did not work out according
to his expectations, but incapable of taking up arms to change
it. Indeed, his tolerant acceptance of a grandson marrying a
convert is a sign that in his old age he had decided to come
to terms with the changes in modern life. Equally remarkable was his participation in the Bat Mitzvah* of his great
grand-daughter who, against all orthodox tradition, read
from the *Torah*, the sacred scroll to celebrate her achievement of puberty by mastering the Hebrew text. He even
criticised his son-in-law, the Bat Mitzvah's father, who was
still very orthodox, for objecting to this break from tradition.

When I told my father that due to his enlightened attitude,
he had become a hero to his granddaughter, the mother of
the Bat Mitzvah, he smiled and said, also in tolerance,
'Norbert is very strict. You know why in the past a woman
shouldn't read publicly from the *Sefer Torah*? It was because
of *kibud tzibur*, respect for the community, for women not to
exhibit themselves. But things were different then. Today,
when women do *everything*, it is the opposite. It gives respect
to the community when a girl reads from the *Sefer Torah*'.

The Abah was not emotionally expressive, and so I
remember vividly the scene when he received that telegram
from Jerusalem in which there were only two transliterated
Hebrew words: '*Abah niftar*, Father has died'. The Abah left
the dining room, where he had read the news to go into the
kitchen. He returned with a large meat knife, inserted its
blade into the top buttonhole of his jacket and cut it through;
cried out and the tears flowed. He had not seen his father for
twenty years, having left Palestine in 1930. I was stunned, as
I had never seen my father cry. I too will cry when I hear the
news in London, because it is unlikely that I will have sufficient forewarning to be at his side when he dies. I will weep
for a man who, while he did not urge me on, did not hold me

---

* A boy is a Bar Mitzvah, son of commandment, a girl is Bat Mitzvah,
daughter of commandment, i.e. both become morally responsible at the
age of puberty.

back; who while he rejected my ways, never rejected me, and who was prepared to let himself be proud of me as a good and loving son, even though I had departed from the charted path set by his ancestors, a path which he too might have left had another been open to him.

I was not by my father's side when he died, but had seen him two weeks before. By this time he was blind which deprived him of reading his sacred texts. He was also incontinent as a result of a cancer for which he refused treatment. He had said to me a few years earlier when he was offered an operation, 'Shimshon in this country they don't let you die'. He had decided that his time had come and was rather upset with God for not realising it as he had. He spent the last months of his life only eating chocolates and drinking Drambuie, the Scottish liquor which I brought him. During my last visit when he was in a semi–coma and I wanted to make an appropriate farewell, he raised his eyes to me and mumbled in good humour 'Shimshon, next time you come, bring the children'.

5

God in my house

The reality of God was never an issue in our home. How could it be otherwise, when we were always praying to him and blessing him, and when my father's livelihood depended on the fact that Jews could only eat chickens, according to the laws of God as handed down by Moses. How could anyone in my family doubt his existence, when he had always been part of our experience? If, for over three thousand years, your ancestors have spoken to him, have lived according to his commands, have explained every event in their history, miracles and disasters according to his being, it is difficult not to believe. True, he was invisible but I had more authoritative evidence for his existence than that the earth was round. If I denied his existence, I might as well have denied the existence of my Zaydeh.

Strangely enough, I had never thought of God as a man with a long white beard. His invisibility and all pervasiveness meant that for me even as a child God could have no body. I might have believed that Elijah the Prophet had an invisible body when he crept into our home to take a sip out of his wine cup at the Passover Seders, but not God. His grandeur could not be limited by a body.

Paradoxically, while his reality was assumed, I felt that he was ignored. He was like an old family retainer whom one takes for granted and whose presence is hardly noticed. Our blessings were said with no more thought than a British person saying 'sorry' when someone steps on his toes. It was almost a reflex. God was around, but as he did not make his presence felt in ordinary day to day life, we felt he did not expect us to give him more than perfunctory acknowledge-

ment. He was like a king who expected you to pay your taxes
but didn't expect you to curtsey before his framed picture
every time you passed it by. He was there, but in reserve,
ready to be called upon for help or condemned for not giving
it.

The special days on which Jews are reminded why they
owe God allegiance, the Sabbath, Festivals, and High Holy
Days, were the most pleasant days in our home. These were
days in which Jews felt special. The rest of the world was
shut out as we celebrated our special relationship with God.
We even managed to forget that in spite of our hot line to
God we were still a despised minority without the power
to defend ourselves. Even on these occasions I felt that our
behaviour, while based on divine commandment, was for our
benefit and not his.

The 'Old Testament' God of justice who instructs the
Children of Israel to clear out Canaan before settling there
was not the God worshiped in our home. From my experience, he was a fun loving God with great understanding and
sympathy for the weaknesses of human beings which he had
created. He was a benevolent despot. What Jews write over
the synagogue arks, which contain their holy scrolls, tells
it all. Some congregations opt for the verse 'Know before
whom you stand!' and some use the verse 'Serve the Lord
with gladness'. Respect and joy was what our God expected,
not the guilt induced by a God who dies for our sins, nor the
God who tells us to conquer the world with the promise of a
sensual paradise, if we should die in the effort.

The God of Abraham, Isaac and Jacob was a very human
God. He made deals with them and they made deals with
him. 'If you worship me and do what I tell you, I will look
after you'. And Jacob responds, 'If you keep your promise
and help me out, I will give you 10%'. He was emotional
about the Jews. He loved them and chose them. He does
crazy things; he promises Abraham to make the descendents
of Isaac as numerous as the sands of the sea and then tells
him to offer the boy up as a sacrifice. Of course, he changes

his mind. When he decides to wipe out the twin cities of sin, Sodom and Gemmora, he feels compelled to tell his major shareholder in the morality business. But Abraham says 'No' because the innocent would suffer with the wicked. They start bargaining.

'Suppose there are fifty good people?'
'Fine, city saved.'
'If there are forty?'
'Right, I'll go along with that too.'
'Ten less – thirty?'
'I'm being soft, but okay.'
'What about twenty?'
'You're pushing your luck but all right.'
'This is my last word and then I'll shut up. How about Ten?'
'It's a deal.'

All the stories about God which I read in the Bible, and the way we celebrated his holidays with good food and wine and dressed up in our best clothes convinced me that the Jewish God was a jolly fellow. I was never told, 'Sidney, be good or God will punish you'. It was only much later that I felt there must be some sanctions he could apply if you broke the rules, but my general impression was that he had bigger fish to fry. His relationship was with the entire Jewish People, and I was only one little minnow in a big sea.

It could have been different though, if I hadn't fluffed it. At least that is what I thought then. I was three years old, and still sleeping in a cot in my parents' room. It was in the middle of the night, I was awakened by a stentorian call, 'Sidney'. It could only be God. I sat up. I was terrified. I screamed, and God went away, and I felt a mixture of relief and sadness. Not long after this nocturnal happening, I was told the story of Samuel's dream. God appeared to him and he, instead of screaming, reported the incident to Eli, the High Priest, who told him what to do the next time God called. The result: Two books in the Bible entitled Samuel I and Samuel II. There will never be a Shimshon I and a Shimshon II. I had a chance to make history but proved myself unworthy.

If I have faltered in my faith over the years, it is because all the miracles that God worked to get us out of Egypt and into the Promised Land were overshadowed by his silence in Auschwitz, Treblinka and in all the towns of Eastern and Western Europe. God lost some credibility. How I managed to adjust my faith so that he could continue to remain my God is another matter, but I will always regret never knowing what would have happened if I had not, in my fright, driven God away.

6

The war and blowing bubbles

The black window blind was rolled down only once in the kitchen, during an air-raid alarm. It was only down for ten minutes before the all-clear signal was heard. That was the only sound of war I heard. We knew only one soldier who lived in the apartment on the floor below. My older brother was studying at Yeshiva University when the war began. My sister was about fifteen and had no friends who became soldiers. The war seemed very distant, and was fought on movie screens and in children's war games. War songs were all pervasive. Patriotic songs like 'Remember Pearl Harbour', 'Anchors away, my boy, anchors away' were constantly on our lips. 'You're a sap Mr Jap' and other songs intended to dehumanise the enemy were also popular but not as much as the martial tunes.

I know that there were rationing books but I don't recall any shortage of clothing or food. Whatever lack of luxuries we endured, I attributed to our financial situation and not to the war effort.

There seemed no question that we would win the war, and it was only a matter of time before Hitler and Hirohito would surrender. We children were not aware of the destruction, atrocities and suffering happening in Europe and Asia. Without television, we were ignorant of the nature of the violence. The war was one of principle. It did not register that people were dying for these principles. Every morning at the beginning of class, we would rise and say in unison, 'We declare our allegiance to the flag of the United States of America and to the Republic for which it stands, one nation indivisible and liberty and justice for all'. We used to stretch our right arm to point to the 'Stars and Stripes' but this ceased to be the custom because it was to similar to the heil Hitler salute.

In our games, we use to argue as to who should be Eisenhower or MacArthur. I preferred MacArthur. Eisenhower was a great chap, but he had said nothing as admirable as: 'I shall return'. To keep the game going, we had to take turns being the enemy, but we never were able to identify sufficiently with the enemy to fight with any resistance, so we quickly surrendered in order to change parts. It was all very boring, and we often decided that Cowboys and Indians or cops and robbers were capable of more excitement and creativity.

As usual, I had a handicap in these games as well. The Abah and Ima did not approve of war, so I was never bought a toy gun. I was thus dependent on my friends for the temporary loan of a spare pistol. Whatever fun there may have been in the games was greatly diminished by my not even being able to call my gun my own.

But war could never take the place of ball games, and I am still amazed at the inventiveness of children living in the crowded inner city in creating ball games. There was Wire Ball, which consisted of kids standing on the pavements of street corners where telephone or electricity poles reached forty feet in the sky, and the wires would join the two poles on both corners with the street in between. The objective was to throw the rubber ball vertically in the air to reach the height of the wires and then to catch it for a point. If you hit a wire and you were still able to catch it, in spite of the deflection it caused, you got three points. This was a challenging game, as you had to keep an eye on traffic. In those days there were not that many cars but, even when the street was clear and the ball thrown, you had to have a good look before running into the street to catch the ball on its descent. It was considered real rotten luck if you hit a wire and then couldn't catch the ball because a car got in the way.

Another ingenious game was Kerb or Step ball. In our

neighbourhood, the houses were attached and with the exception of a few gardens which separated the clusters of houses, the walls were all in a line, made of brick and cement. There were tiny porches reached by four or five steps. Around the four-foot-square porch, there were nine-inch-wide benches on which one could barely sit and watch if one were not playing. A cement ledge separated the cement from the brick and this was about three feet from the ground. One would stand in the street of the kerb and throw the rubber or tennis ball against the wall. If it bounced and you caught it, you got a point. If it hit the ledge it would create a flier or a liner. If you caught that you scored ten points. That was not always so easy, as the ball could fly out at an angle or go into the street and you had to be warned about passing cars and trolley cars. And of course, there was always catch. Tennis balls were thrown overhand, underhand and sidehand. Each of us sought to emulate the baseball pitchers of the Phillies or the 'A's baseball teams. The streets were sufficiently narrow so 'catches' took place between two sides of the streets. The richer kids had baseball gloves, so they could take the sting out of the 'catch' and at the same time add to their fantasy by catching the balls in the pocket of their glove single-handed, if the ball was thrown hard enough and you closed your glove at the right moment.

In addition to these games there was Hose Ball. Water hoses were cut into three inch segments and hit by a broom-stick handle. If you could hit the hose into the sky without it being caught, or you hit it on the ground a certain distance, you achieved a single; a longer distance, a double; an even longer distance, a triple. If you could hit it over a house, that was a home run. The swish of the bat hitting the hose and the whistling noise the hose made as it went through the air was a beautiful sound, and being a funny kind of ball, because of its rectangular dimensions, you never knew where it would go. I need not tell you that there was a special art for throwing such a ball. Only the cleverest kids made a mark for themselves in this game.

So it was during the war: to school and back home, a glass of milk and a chocolate cup cake, some homework and out to play. The girls did not play anything but hopscotch or skipping rope. Sometimes the boys joined in the more challenging rope games. I hated them. Two children would hold the rope and the others would jump across them and each time they cleared it, the rope was raised slightly higher and the winner was the one who cleared the highest. There were many arguments. 'Hey, you raised the rope higher when I jumped'. 'I did not!' 'You did too'. Most kids didn't like to hold the rope, but since I was not a good jumper, I would be the good sport until my hand would ache from being in the same position. Hopscotch was a game played both by boys and girls, but the real fun was the excitement of chalking out the lines and numbering the boxes.

There were numerous card games, like War, or Fish or Steal the old man's bundle, but the only indoor game I remember with excitement was Monopoly. I had heard of games such as Spin the bottle but as these were kissing games, I only saw them through the cracks in the door and saw little kissing but heard much tittering. Monopoly was different. While I begged to be allowed to be an independent player I ended up in partnership with my sister who made all the decisions. Still, being allowed to move the tokens and to identify with her was a thrill. I would dream of building hotels on Boardwalk and Park Avenue. I looked forward to being protected in jail while others landed on our properties and we could not land on theirs. There was joy as you picked up hundreds from your opponent and misery as you de-housed your properties to pay off with the grim knowledge that once stripped, your fortunes, perhaps like real life, would never rise again.

At night, as I lay in bed, waiting for my sister to join me [she was fifteen years old, I was five, and she shared a bed with me in our two-bed roomed flat until we moved] I would fantasize. Usually, I fell asleep before she got into bed, but while I was awake I imagined myself a general of boy soldiers

leading my troops into war and to victory. As I dreamt
dreams, I would move my lips across the tiny hairs on my
arm to give me physical comfort. Those fantasies ended
when the war ended and we moved to a new house.

During sultry summer evenings, when we sat on the porch
or on the steps and applied cold wet compresses over our
foreheads and necks to wipe away the sweat of the humid
Philadelphia air, the older girls and boys indulged in sexy
stories and innuendos. I remember my puzzlement when a
boy lit a paper match to demonstrate the state of penis after
an erection. 'What is an erection?' I asked innocently. The
response was sardonic laughter. The girls would swap glossy
8" by 10" pictures of movie stars Clark Gable, Lana Turner,
Gregory Peck, Alan Ladd and Betty Grable.

The war caused me little hardship. Life went on rather
normally. The crazy old black lady would walk down 8th
Street, periodically stamping one foot and slapping herself
against the face. We kids would speak of her as a witch and
wait terrified as she would approach, but the terror was of
our own creation. She had a greater influence on our lives
than did Hitler with his troops overrunning Europe.

I must correct myself. There was one hardship I remember. Due to the war effort, there was a great scarcity of Fleers
double-bubble gum. It could not be purchased for love or
money. Suddenly the word would go out and spread like wild
fire. A new supply was at the candy store. We would all run
home, pick up our pennies, rush to the shop. By the time I
arrived, it was all gone.

One day a friend drew me aside and told me that his
friend's father was a grocer and that he had a full box of
bubble gum. That meant a box holding 144 pieces. He had
asked his friend for a piece who had agreed and as a sign of
friendship, my friend was going to let me share in his good
fortune if the piece ever materialised. For days I would say to
my friend, 'Well?' The reply was, 'He says tomorrow while
his Dad is out'. Tomorrow came and passed as did other
tomorrows. Finally, my friend told me that 'tomorrow' had

come. Together we joined the boy and walked respectfully to his dark flat. He took the key from underneath the mat, opened the door, went into the dining room, got on a chair, removed the box from the top of the closet, put it on the table, extracted one piece which measured one half inch in length, took a knife and cut it in half, slicing not only the pink bubble gum, but the comic strip which covered it. Ceremoniously he handed us both our half pieces, swore us to secrecy, and we left deferentially, waiting for the right precious moment to put the juicy double-bubble gum into our mouth. So impressed on my memory was the anticipation of the pleasure of chewing that gum and blowing bubbles, that I do not remember the reality of actually doing it.

Though I lived through the war, it only became important to me when I was old enough to appreciate its consequences. It was to change my world, but how was I to know that at a time when what counted was being able to blow bubbles when others couldn't.

7

The Zionist Dream

I had turned nine when, coming home from school, I heard that the war had ended. My father was speaking with shock of what had happened to the Jews in Europe. Compounded with that memory was the fact that Jews in Palestine were fighting the British and Arabs for a State of their own. I did not know then how these two phenomena, the Holocaust and Israel were to continue to have the greatest affect upon me as they changed Jewish history. But they coalesced to the memory of *one* event which must have reached deeply into my soul. It was when I heard two Irish kids on a bus referring to a recent attack against the British by the Jewish 'underground'. One said to the other: 'You know, those damned Jews can fight.' Suddenly I felt that as a Jew I was part of the human race. the two Irish lads had confirmed that Jews could be like the rest of humanity, not automatic victims. I was no longer a total outsider!

Thus I became a Zionist at the best of all possible times. Others had dreamed the Zionist dream for decades, attended international conferences, argued about and came to blows on Zionist objectives. If Palestine was not available, what about Uganda as an alternative? On this issue, the architect of modern Zionism, Theodore Herzl was to lose the leadership of the movement he created. Not for me the dreams or debates. For me it was to be the reality and I was to get in on the ground floor.

In 1947, I was seduced into joining the *Shomer Hadati*, 'The Religious Guardian' Zionist Youth Club in Logan. This was the orthodox response to the Kibbutz movement. *Torah v'Avodah*, 'The Law and manual labour' was its motto.

Pure communism was wedded to Torah, and both were to be rooted in the redemption of the wasteland of the Holy Land.

For a child of eleven, this had little relevance. What was important was the guts it took to walk alone during a dark evening into the Community Hall of the Conservative synagogue where there would be other children I had never seen who were being roped in as was I to form the new Logan Branch.

Longing as I was for companionship, I took the leap and went. Before I knew what was happening, I was in a circle doing 'sissy' dances to the tunes of Eastern European folk songs expropriated by the Zionists for their own pleasure. The designated girl would sing the refrain of the tune and, amidst clapping, walk around the inner circle. When the refrain finished, she would stop before the boy of her choice and beckon him with her forefinger to join him in the circle for a dance. Protocol demanded that he shyly shake his head thrice in refusal while she beckoned thrice using her forefinger in the most seductive fashion. The formalities being satisfied, with the encouragement of his and her mates, they would join and cross their right arms, do a spin around and separate. It was now his turn to walk around and select an 'unwilling' partner until everyone in the circle was eliminated. They then all joined hands and spun around in a *hora*.

The ordeal of 'sissy' dances was the price to be paid for joining the orthodox Jewish pioneers, who were to provide the religious foundation for the Jewish Commonwealth, reborn after 2000 years. In retrospect, it does indicate the easy going nature of orthodoxy in those days. I doubt very much whether today, boys and girls in the same youth groups – they still exist – would be permitted to dance together. It would be considered immodest and though innocent enough, could lead to 'bad habits' and the 'wrong mental set'.

As a child of eleven, theoretical debates had little impact on me. Growing up was enough of a problem for me to take very seriously any attempts of the leader to persuade me that every good Jew belonged in Israel, and that I had been recruited for that purpose. I had my own problems in the present. My personal attainment of becoming a teenager was more real for me than the need to dedicate my life to guarantee the survival of the Jewish State. Fortunately to compensate for the irrelevancy of Zionist arguments, the Jewish State was about to happen.

Preparations were being made even in Philadelphia for the declaration of an independent Jewish State, and the war that would follow. I was involved in collection days. On a Sunday we would go from door to door with our round tin charity boxes, saying, as the door opened, 'Would you like to support the Jewish State?' Often the door would be silently closed, but sometimes not before we had time to notice faces transfixed with amazement and bewilderment. It could be that I would have looked no different were some lanky Irish children to knock on my door and ask for support for an independent Northern Ireland. I felt, as did my mates, very courageous as we went collecting. Rejection is never nice, and while Logan had a goodly number of Jews, it was not a Jewish neighbourhood, and the odds against success were very high. A friendly refusal was welcomed. A quarter gave delight, a paper note was ecstasy. The contribution of five dollars would be like drawing a straight flush in poker. As we would approach a block of homes, we would consider how Jewish a street it was. If we knew someone who lived there, we were encouraged believing that Jews stick together. Some streets seemed so unfriendly that we would ring the bell, wait only a few seconds and run on to the next door, hoping that we would be spared rejection. As all the homes were terraced, people would come to the door after we had flitted, and think that mischievous boys were ringing their bells gratuitously. They would never know that because of our cowardice, they had missed the opportunity to do their bit for the fulfilment of the Zionist dream.

On the eve of Israel's Independence, all Zionist youth went collecting for packaged foods to send off to Israel in preparation for her struggle. After a Sunday's effort, we came to our meeting point laden with cans of soup, beans, tuna, salmon, anchovies and juices. That evening we met at a large warehouse to assemble cardboard cartons and to pack the tins into them. We worked and sweated until 11:00 pm. The warehouse was only dimly lit intensifying the impression that we were involved in some clandestine enterprise. We quenched our thirst by drinking gallons of juice intended for Jewish soldiers. We justified this as an administrative expense. Our talk was of the rich Jews who had provided the warehouse and the cartons and were hiring the ships, some said from Czechoslovakia, to deliver the food as well as arms to the Jewish State, which would soon be under siege.

The sense of illegality about what we were doing added to the excitement and made us feel at one with those Jews who had smuggled illegal immigrants into Palestine and had broken British resistance to the creation of a Jewish homeland. American Jews had no reason to feel this way, but somehow, the U.S., in spite of its support for the Zionist dream, was still part of the world, and could anyone doubt that basically the world was against the Jews? Was there not the expectation that the Arabs would crush the baby nation at its birth? A bad conscience that the U.S. had not taking more Jews out of the Nazi inferno, and not bombed the trains or the camps was motivation for most Americans to want the Jews to have a country of their own, but the guilt and shame was not great enough to guarantee the Jews would actually achieve it. The Jews would have to fight for Israel's survival on their own. This message was never conveyed to me as part of my Zionist training. I attribute it to the inheritance of acquired characteristics, even though it is a theory of Freud which has been rejected as unscientific.

Leaping forward, beyond my youth, into my personal and Jewish history, this mood repeated itself before the Six Day War. Jews thought that with the withdrawal of UN Forces in the Straits of Tiran and the lack of guarantees by the Western Powers, Israel would be pushed into the Sea. Non-Jews felt the same way. The only difference being that while

Diaspora Jews were in helpless agony, declaring that defeat and destruction would destroy what remained of their Jewish faith, non-Jews did not care very much. A few were relishing the prospect of sending out boats in a grand humanitarian effort to save Jewish mothers and children. Had the war ended as anticipated, Jews would have returned to their rightful place in history, as victims of human aggression, and scapegoats for human failings, and as proof of the truth of the Pauline Christian message that mankind was rotten through and through and could only be redeemed through the grace of a dying God. Ironically, this God, who came from the bosom of the Jews, was rejected by them, and it was they who, according to the Gospels were responsible for his death, while Pontius Pilate washed his hands of guilt.

What Jew, alive at the time, does not remember the sense of the miraculous when Israel achieved almost instant victory in the first day of the War! The Sabbath following June 6, Jews went in vast numbers to their synagogues to sing songs of thanksgiving to their God who had not been witness to such a victory since the successful crossing of the Red Sea. Jews, who had lost their faith during and after the Holocaust, saw the hand of God transforming their lives. Living in a period of non-belief, they did not have the vocabulary to explain it to themselves. It was a wonder beyond the power of articulation. Post-holocaust theologians were to write about it as the rebirth of the divine presence in human history.

Back to my Zionist childhood: I can also credit Zionism with first stimulating romantic feelings within me. Because I did not identify with such singers as Bing Crosby or Frank Sinatra, their love songs never moved me. The songs from *State Fair* and *Oklahoma* were different. Though stirred by them, I could not envisage myself in the situation of those with booming, voices reflecting their power over life and the hearts of beautiful and rosy cheeked all-American girls. These were not fantasies appropriate to a poor little Jewish boy.

It was around the campfire, organized by a group in

Fairmount Park that notions of romance entered my head. After the hot dogs had been eaten, and the talks on the glories of Judaism and the Jewish State duly delivered, the singing began. Among the songs devoted to Zion were those based on verses of the *Songs of Solomon*, 'My beloved is mine and I am his; the sound of my lover approaches, skipping upon the hills, jumping over the high ridges; I went down to the orchard of nuts to see if the vines had blossomed', were three such songs which lifted my spirits and made me feel that this was my kind of loving. The love between a shepherd and his lass in the pastures of Judea expressed in classical Hebrew was an emotional event with which I could identify. Others quoted Shakespeare or John Donne to their girl friends. I would sing the *Song of Songs* to mine.

Zionism became an integrating force in the development of my character. Love of the Jewish People, love of the land of its prophets and kings and the love of a dream of a people's redemption from servility and humiliation combined with my own hope that, when I was grown up, I too would love and be loved by a woman with the grace of that 'lily of the valley' who rejected the king's advances because she preferred the simple shepherd Jewish boy whom she had loved since childhood.

8

Physical Cowardice and Mental Courage

It has been said that one's character is one's fate. I think that my birth was instrumental in forging my character. I was born at Mt Sinai hospital in South Philadelphia. Not only did I suffer the trauma of birth to which the psychoanalyst, Adler, attributed most anxieties and neuroses, I was also born with a hernia in my groin.

I am told that I was a beautiful baby with golden curly locks, enough to make passers-by stop in admiration as I was wheeled along in my pram. This outward grace disappeared when I was one year old. I was to have an operation on my hernia. In those days, the mother was not allowed to go into hospital with the child. I was wrenched away weeping from my mother, and a day later I was returned to her, all the curls gone, but the hernia still there. The doctors, having failed in the operation, now advised that because of my frailty, it would be best to wait until I was older before another operation was attempted. This meant that until I was fifteen I had to live with nagging discomfort and a disability which was to limit my physical development. It is always painful to be hit in the private parts but when it happened to me, the pain was more intense and lasted longer.

Running and engaging in sport was not pleasurable. I was skinny and, due to lack of exercise, the little flesh I had was non muscular. I looked like the before of the 'before and after' advertisement for a weight lifting course. At an early age, I was reconciled to the fact that not being in the position to turn the tables on the bully, I would have to learn how to avoid his bravado. This reconciliation to my weakness appears to have had an impact upon my general attitude to challenges. I try, but not to the point of obsession. I admit failure more readily than most and don't shore up my self-confidence by pretending success when there is none. To survive, I learned to live with my weaknesses, to admit to them and to work around them.

However unpleasurable for me, Physical Training (PT) was part of the school curriculum, and engaging in sports was the only way for me to have a social life. Imagine my situation during a glorious summer afternoon in Fairmount Park, across the road from the school I attended. Two captains were chosen for a soccer or softball game. The captains tossed for who would choose first from all the players. When only two hapless boys remained to be chosen, the captains would determine who had the strongest side and for the sake of fairness put me on it to give the game the right balance. How I cringed in embarrassment as my mates congratulated themselves on their fairness while morally crushing me at the same time. I remember with delight the day that a player worse than me was found, and it was he and not I who was considered the weakest player. It was as though I had won an Olympic Gold. I used to fantasize about making a great catch or hitting a home run. In a real game, my major objective was not to be a hero but to avoid screwing it up for my side, or at least not to be blamed for doing it. This anxiety made me, when fielding, and I was always put into the outfield because there was far less action there, seek to avoid the place where the ball might come. I had decided that the rebuke, 'Where were you, Sidney?' was better than all eyes on me as a high flying ball fell in and out of my hands. On the rare occasion when the ball could not be avoided, and I actually caught it, I was a hero, and would radiate in my success for days. I never did hit a home run, but once hit a double. When I did hit the ball, I ran as quickly as I could, but because of my hernia I never listened to my mates urging me to slide safely into base to avoid the touch of the ball in the fielder's mitt, which would have meant that I was 'out'.

I could have avoided all this embarrassment by saying, 'I don't wanna play'. I had a class mate who never played. He was a tall lanky fellow who was a bird watcher. During free time, he would go with his binoculars into the park and look at birds. But he was considered an oddball. I was gregarious, and was prepared to suffer the anguish of shame in order to be where the action was.

But I had no physical self confidence. Even though I was not a bad catcher, the fear that the ball would hit me between the legs terrified me, and this fear caused me to drop it. This was called not being good in the clutch. Because of my physical handicap, fright in the face of physical challenge became second nature. To take a dare to jump across a stream meant nothing to other children, except the possibility of wet shoes and trousers if they failed and glory if they succeeded. To me, the least it meant was wet clothing and a scolding from my mother. The worst was pain and greater injury. I don't know why I did not justify my physical limitations by explaining my situation. Perhaps one did not speak about one's private areas. Also I never knew what a hernia actually was. Because I had it since birth, it was assumed that in the course of growing up, someone must have told me, but no one ever did; so my defect was a mystery even to me.

My body was an embarrassment to me. In my cousin's home they had full length wall mirrors in the bathroom: I used to look at my legs and could not believe how thin they were. Perhaps, the mirrors lied, but no, 'Sidney had concentration legs' was the quip that greeted me, as I ventured forth from the dressing room to the side of the swimming pool or onto the beach. It would be difficult for me to assess how much mental anguish I suffered every time I anticipated the need to reveal my physical being, but it was a major part of my emotional life.

This utter lack of confidence in my body, combined with fear of pain, made me a physical coward. While other children looked for adventures, I ran away from them. I once fell off a bike and grazed myself. Because of this minor incident I was frightened when my cousins – we were about six at the time – told me that a big kid on their block was giving rides on his bicycle to the younger children and that we could take turns riding on the handlebars, I said, 'Fine', but terrified crept away and hid at the back of the house for what seemed like hours. When I could no longer bear the suspense or the boredom and decided to make my appearance, my cousins told me that they had been looking all over for me because my turn had come up, but it was too late because the boy had gone home with his bike.

As I had no hope of achieving any distinction athletically or by feats of physical prowess, I had to show my mettle in another way. My mental courage took me by surprise! The congressional election in 1946 had favoured the Republicans, much to the dismay of my father who was a Trade Unionist and a Democrat. My battle axe of a teacher in the Ludlow State school preened herself on the Republican victory and felt the need to ventilate her joy to a class of ten-year-olds. She asked, 'Anyone sad about the election?' With disbelief I saw my hand rise as though of its own volition, and before I could lower it, she called upon me. I rose to my feet and found myself saying, 'Well, I am not exactly sad about it, but I'm not exactly happy about it either', and sat down. There was no response from her but I have reason to believe that when she caught me whispering to my neighbour a week later, her hauling me to her desk and shaking me harshly by my shoulders was her way of punishing me for my political dissidence.

At that moment, I discovered the thrill of increased adrenalin flow and a pounding heart when one spoke up for a dangerous cause. I began to defend the actions of class-mates in which I had not been involved. While there was always the possibility of punishment, I knew that it would not be physical or at least it would not be a kick in the balls. My willingness to buck authority made me quite popular.

My friends could not quite understand how such a weed had guts, and some even believed that I must also have physical courage since they could not discriminate between the two. This induced me to pretend that I was not easily frightened. Once, only once, I hit a big kid on the chin with my fist. I don't remember the reason. He was stunned not by my strength but by surprise. Before he recovered and picked himself off from the ground, I told him that it was an accident. Why he let it pass, I do not know, but I counted my lucky stars that he did. The risk in displaying moral or intellectual courage became my substitute for the normal adventures of childhood. Moral brinkmanship took the place of leaping from one side of the stream to the other.

I was never foolhardy. I believed in risk limitation. That meant the use of persuasion rather than bravado. In situations of conflict, I would seek to blur the issues by showing that there were two sides. The achievement of a compromise with authorities was in my view a victory. I enjoyed many such minor triumphs and I was helped by the confusion caused in the opposition by the sight of a frightened-looking little kid respectfully but eloquently arguing causes. My success gave me confidence and I learnt that survival and status could be achieved without physical strength if one acted intelligently and with a clear purpose of mind. I now consider it remarkable that the circumstances of my own birth should have led me, in my own life, to play the same role as played by the Jewish people in their efforts to survive over centuries of dispersion. This may be yet another reason why I feel so comfortable with my Jewishness and gladly accept, perhaps out of necessity, a condition which most run miles to avoid.

9

Sensual Pleasure and
Moral Lessons in Atlantic City

'You can't look neat if your shoes look beat', was the cry of the enterprising black manager of a shoeshine stall along the Boardwalk. Even though I knew that my shoes had been meticulously polished by my mother, I always had to look at my shoes to see whether I was neat or beat. In the '40s and '50s, Atlantic City was Philadelphia's playground. It had a boardwalk stretching for five miles along pure white sandy beaches which could be reached by walking down about five wooden steps. The beach under the boardwalk was usually littered with cans, ice lolly sticks and the remnants of sexual exploits.

For years I thought it was called 'Etlentic City', because that was the way it was pronounced by the Jews who went there for a day trip or spent a week or more in some dingy rooming house or rented flat. Atlantic City, however, served all classes. There was the prosperous section with its stately hotels by the Boardwalk. You knew you had walked a very long way on the five-mile Boardwalk when one reached the Claremont Hotel with its beautiful garden and water fountain which changed colours. We would stop there and gaze in wonder at the world of the rich. It never occurred to us to leave the Boardwalk and meander into its lobby. It would have required the same arrogance as going into an emperor's palace uninvited. On the one hand were the poor who walked to the beach laden with blankets, towels, chairs, umbrellas, picnic lunches and sighed a sigh of relief when they dropped their burden at their destination; on the other, there were the

rich who unencumbered walked from the hotel to their
pre-booked Cabana with only a towel casually slung over
their shoulders.

When I heard that I was to go on vacation to 'Etlentic
City', I never thought to ask in what style. For me a vacation
was not related to 'stars of quality' for accommodation. A
vacation by the seaside was something I *never* imagined I
would ever enjoy. It appeared that it was because of me that
we were going on vacation. The doctor had said that Atlantic
City, [I am sure he pronounced it correctly] was the best
place for my allergic asthma. The sea air and the lower pollen
count would help me survive the hayfever season.

Can anyone who has not suffered from asthma know what
it means to be constantly gasping for breath and never knowing when, if ever, the attack was going to end? This was in
the days before Ventilin and Bectosil inhalants. Asthma is
not like pain, because it doesn't hurt. It is just a matter of not
being able to get what you need. Shouting and crying do not
help and are not even possible because you are too busy trying to breathe. Nor can you blame anyone. The air is there. It
is your own inadequacy not to be able to catch hold of it.
How I suffered and what thoughts went through my mind I
cannot explain at those times when God did not deign to
breathe into me the life he was able to give to Adam and his
other descendents. When it became really bad and there were
panic signals, I was given a Ventolin pill. In thirty minutes or
so, I would hear my heart beginning to pound and I knew
that relief was on the way. My heart had been stimulated,
was working harder. My lungs had expanded and the air
flowed in. It was a strange feeling. My body felt like a bell
over which I had no control. My heart was beating like
chimes with such a resounding noise that I was afraid my
body would crack from the pounding. By that time, however,
it did not matter. I could breathe. I could fall into a blissful
sleep.

I was nine when we made our first trek to Atlantic City. I
remember my mother and me trudging by bus and train.

From the Atlantic City train station we took a taxi to the boarding house. It was a house with a wide porch in which there were rows of wooden rocking chairs. Our bedroom was small: place for one chest of drawers, a two-foot space between my mother's three-foot wide-bed and my two-foot-six wide-divan bed. I did not care. I urged my mother to hurry up. The time she took unpacking seemed like hours. She then wanted to go food shopping so she could make us some sandwiches for the beach. 'Please, Ima, let's go now, we'll have ice cream on the beach.' I had heard from my friends that men carrying ice cream boxes on their backs came by every few minutes. She relented and we were on our way. So, clad in bathing suits and dressing gowns, with a few rolls which she had brought from Philadelphia, in case of emergency, two towels and a beach blanket we made the ten minute walk to the beach.

We must have been a strange pair as we walked onto the beach for the first time in my life: a bent-over forty-five-year-old woman, looking more like sixty, and a skinny under-nourished looking-child of nine. I was aware of my self consciousness and wondered whether they would allow us onto the beach at all. No one took any notice of us. It was in the afternoon and most of those on the beach had already had a morning of sun, sand and sea, had eaten lunch and were too enervated by swimming and beach athletics to notice anything.

Sure enough, by the time we had buried the four corners of the blanket in the sand to keep it from blowing over, I heard the ice cream-man calling out, 'Ice cream cones, ice lollies, all flavours, 10 cents!' How he managed to carry that heavy ice-box along the hot sands, I never understood. It taught me that there were people even poorer than my father, compelled to do such hard work to make a living. At that time, I was too eager to feel the water under my feet to ask for an ice cream. But, on the occasions that I ran to him, I felt that my purchase was important not only because of my yearning for its refreshing qualities but because it enabled the poor man to rest the box on the sand while he gave me the ice cream. This must have been more important at that moment than making the sale.

If you are wondering if I really had such thoughts at the time, the answer is that I *was* thinking them. I didn't have much else to do with my time than to think. In my home, thinking was very respectable. On occasion when my mother had not noticed me around for a while and would call, 'Shimshon,, what are you doing', I would often reply, 'Nothing Ima, just thinking'. And she would say, 'Fine' and return to her labour. I *thought* of the ice cream seller, and I *thought* of those boys and girls doing somersaults and callisthenics on the beach and I wondered how it could be so easy for them? How did one get such a beautiful body, and how did it feel to move blithely along the beach on sturdy limbs, able to jump in the water, without giving a thought to its shivering quality or the shells which could cut into your feet? These were for me the 'untouchables'; nothing could hurt them.

On my first day at the beach, I did not think. I just wanted to get my feet wet. I promised not to go fully into the water but just to get a feel of it and my mother, with this assurance, let me go off on my own. I couldn't believe how cold it was, but the combination of sand and water going between my toes was a delight I will never forget. The disappearing sound of the tiny breakers as they licked my toes was also very reassuring. I got lost in the pleasure and felt that it had all been created for me, waiting there nine years for me to dip my feet in. I rushed back and asked permission to go up to my knees. Permission granted, I braved the cold, went up to my knees and sat down in the water, turned over on my tummy and came in with the waves. For me it was heaven, reciprocal love between me and the ocean. The water stroked me as my mother never had. The ocean taught me sensualism. The sand taught me the pleasures of wallowing in it without guilt, because *even* my mother could not accuse me of getting dirty when I was covered in wet mushy sand. Ocean, sand and the sun's warmth gave me back a babyhood, which I think I was never quite allowed to enjoy. The Ima's boast that as a baby I was never dirty proves this point. My toilet training must have started at day one. No wonder then at my ecstasy at being covered by the ocean waves or able to bury myself in the sand! My wise sister-in-law, advising me against prudery and inhibition, once said, 'You have not lived until you've taken off your shoes and run barefoot on the grass'. My sensual life and my delight in my body began when I first enjoyed being stroked by the sea, dirtied by the sand and dried out by the loving sun.

After my first day at the beach, I returned elated to the room. I endured a bath and a hair wash in a dank smelly bathroom with sand in the tub, which resisted all my attempts to push them down the drain. After the pure baptism of the sea, I felt sullied by the bath. But as I got dressed into well-pressed short-sleeved shirt and trousers, I felt good. I still felt caressed by the sea and the sun. My face was pink rather than pallid, and as I looked into the mirror above the chest of drawers, I felt I was looking at a lovelier boy than the one who had arrived from Philadelphia that morning. We had a sandwich supper. I don't think my mother used the shared kitchen and dining room to make anything but sandwiches. One of the benefits of the vacation was that she was not going to cook. My sister, middle brother and the Abah in Philadelphia would have to cook for themselves.

After supper, it was with great anticipation that we approached the Boardwalk. We joined it at the undeveloped part, which was unadorned by shops or stalls. The ocean side was totally uncluttered with the exception of two pleasure piers, which gave us a constant view of the rushing sea. It was not long before we came to the souvenir shops, shoeshine and ice cream palours, 'pokerino'* and penny arcades and small

* For 10 cents, a dime, you get five balls which you roll down an alley, aiming for holes to achieve a good poker hand, resulting in monetary rewards.

halls where hawkers sold miracle cures and gadgets on commission. I was not disappointed. It was a world lit up with
people. The older people, in my mind those over forty,
walked with great seriousness as if they were meeting an
obligation to give their bodies a 'constitutional' after eating
too much. The teenagers jostled each other as they laughed
and pointed to this or that thing of interest. Children were
dragging their parents to the shops, spying something,
which they just *had* to have. For me it was life and life more
abundant.

What really amazed me, however, was the cushioned
wickered chairs on two big wheels in which grown-ups were
pushed along by black men. The long handle bar was no
more than a foot length from the back of the chair so the
sedentary occupants literally had the black men breathing
down their necks. What luxury, I thought, but it gave me a
queasy feeling. I longed to be pushed along the Boards like a
little emperor, indicating with a gesture of my hand a scene
that caught my interest or my desire for an ice cream or
pretzel. But I knew this was never to be. The Ima confirmed
my own instincts that it was not right for people to earn a
living by doing the walking for others. My father also
thought it was a scandal that there were capitalists who could
take such pleasure in demeaning others. I remember debating
the moral dilemma with my father. 'But Abah, they want to
push you down the Boardwalk. They need the money.
You're doing them a favour'. His reply was, 'If people were
menschen, that is to say decent human beings, they wouldn't
be pushed like this and the *Shvartzes* would find a nicer way
to make a living. '*Es passt nicht zu machen a leben in solchen
veg*', it is unseemly to make a living in such a way. I had to
agree.

Once, however, this principle was broken. One Saturday
night we had walked almost the whole length of the Boardwalk. My mother was seized with a stomach cramp. She
turned to the Abah, who came for the weekends when we
had moved on to renting a summer apartment, '*Shloime, ich*

chalash', Shloime, I am fainting away. What to do? Obviously she couldn't walk back. To leave the Boardwalk and find a taxi would mean a walk of fifteen minutes. Reluctantly, my father concluded that there was no alternative but to be pushed to our end of the Boardwalk. It was a case of *P'kuach Nefesh*, the saving or preservation of life, the highest principle in Judaism to which almost all other values had to be sacrificed, saving three, the destruction of another life, denying God's sovereignty, and incest. The *Shvartze* could be considered like a stretcher-bearer. I was absolutely delighted as my father apologised for giving the driver the fare he was so pleased to have. We all got on. Because my mother was small and frail and I was skinny, he agreed that the Ima and me could count as one. You wont believe it, but after fifty yards or so I felt foolish and embarrassed. People appeared to be looking at us not in admiration, but in disdain as if to say, 'Who do you think you are', or, 'Look at the cripples who can't walk'. I would have gladly jumped off the chair and walked alongside it, had I not originally shown such pleasure at the prospect and urged my father to compromise his principles. Ironically, the Abah now appeared very pleased. Having reconciled himself to the situation, he sat back like to the manner born, talking to the Ima as though they were enjoying their first mischievous escapade in years.

Like the compromise which allowed us to be pushed along the boardwalk, another principle was sacrificed, but this time not for the sake of any higher principle but because I made such an ungodly fuss. The first weekend the Abah arrived, I was told that I couldn't go to the seaside on Saturday because one was not allowed to work on the Sabbath. Carrying anything outside your home was work, ergo, we could not carry the towels and the blanket to the beach. I went berserk. 'It's stupid', I said, 'Why come to Atlantic City if you can't go the beach?' The Abah said, 'What can we do, one is not allowed to carry, the water will be there tomorrow too!' 'But it might rain tomorrow', I cried. When the Abah insisted that the law was the law, I rebelled, 'It's a stupid law, according to the law

you can carry a ton of bricks so long as it is in your house but you're not allowed to carry a handkerchief outside your house. What could be more stupid!' My father pointed out that it was unlikely for people to carry heavy articles in their house but would be inclined to carry objects from one place to another, and how would you logically determine how much was to be permitted? Therefore nothing was allowed. I was not impressed. That whole Sabbath, I sulked and sulked. I had an asthmatic attack. I moaned as though there was no tomorrow.

It worked. The Ima could not cope. 'For this I come on vacation?' she whined. 'He is only a child, not Bar Mitzvah, what difference does it make if he carries?' As usual, the Abah relented and so from then on, when I was on vacation, God too took a holiday. The following Saturday, off I went on my own to the beach, with towel and blanket. The only disadvantage was that I had to watch the ice cream-man go by. He looked at me, expecting to be called on to stop, but on the Sabbath, Jews don't buy or sell, so I had no money. We were both the losers, he without the sale and the moment of respite, and me without the ice cream.

Abah had argued that because I was under thirteen years old and not morally culpable for breaking the *mitzvot*, commandments, he would be held responsible and judged for it in *Olam Haba*, the World-to-Come. The Ima countered, 'Don't worry, Shloime, let it be on my head'. She was a short sighted pragmatist: better to suffer in the World-to-Come for giving in to Sidney than to suffer in this world for *not* giving in to him.

One Sabbath, in our small apartment in Atlantic City, God ceased to take a holiday, because the Zaydeh had arrived. Why he came I do not know. He did not suffer from asthma! He had no intention of going to the beach! He would not even change into summer clothes! *De rigeur*, he wore his three-quarter Prince Edward jacket. He came, he went to *shul*, he studied, he ate, said the many blessings, spoke about the religious politics he had left behind in Philadelphia and the rabbinic hierarchy in Atlantic City. I did not know what to do. With the Zaydeh I could not argue nor would he be amenable to my anger. The Zaydeh could not be offended, nor would he understand my priorities. The Ima came up with a Biblical solution. Like Rebecca coming to the aid of Jacob, her favourite son, by suggesting he trick his ailing father Isaac [who must have been suffering from cataracts not to know that he was not his older brother, Esau] I was advised to slip out while he took a Sabbath nap, and not come back until he went to *shul* in the afternoon which would be an hour and a half before sunset. It was one of the rare occasions when I felt that my Ima had come up trumps, and I loved her for it.

The Zaydeh said something that weekend which left an imprint on me. He was having a glass of milk. He lifted the glass, looked at it and at the remaining milk in the bottle resting on the kitchen table, and said to me, quoting from the Bible in Hebrew 'Shimshon, *Eretz z'vat chalav oo d'vash*, a land flowing with milk and honey, is not a description of Israel, it is a description of America: a golden country'. I am not sure whether he was expressing a subtle rebuke of the Holy One for not giving his chosen people the U.S.A. instead of Canaan or whether he was doubting the accuracy of the holy text. Whatever he was implying, it was the only time I heard him wilfully question God's providence and it gave me an inward smile and further justification for the rebellious streak within me.

Before Atlantic City became the gambling centre of the East Coast, but some years after my annual vacations there, I took a day trip and noticed a great change in the quality of the Boardwalk. Instead of roller chairs, there were motorised chairs. The individuals who drove them no longer sweated but had the look of entrepreneurs rather than slaves. Those being driven looked more like people too tired to walk rather than the bourgeoisie who enjoyed the *schadenfreude* of being moved by the sweat of an inferior's brow. Social democracy, the result of increased wealth and mechanisation had come to the U.S. Other changes had taken place too. There weren't that many pleading to polish your shoes; the hawkers who had entertained us by telling us that olive oil was useless compared to lanolin in retaining one's hair because as he said, 'Have you ever seen hair grow on an olive?' were also gone. The commission on selling cars and TV's must have been greater, no matter how many jars he could sell.

My memories of Atlantic City are bitter sweet. Sweet because there I discovered that my body was capable of pleasure and I was glad of being in possession of it, even though I would have been far happier if it had been my luck to have been given a better one. Sweet, because on those occasions when I found a friend, or my cousins joined me for a weekend, I could share the pleasures of the water and sand and thus increase them. Sweet, because I learnt how to jump the waves and even dive into them on the upturn, without fear, because I was willing to take the risk of being drenched in the sea with the confidence that the loving waves would bring me back to safety. Bitter because the others on the beach seemed to have so much more solidity than did I, so much more self assurance. They made larger imprints in the sand upon which they strutted, while my feet hardly left a mark. Bitter because I was alone so much of the time, miserable when the weather was too wet or cool for sunbathing or swimming and all I could do was walk alone on the empty Boardwalk knowing that it would be hours until it would open up and light itself up with the life of bustling humanity. On those days when I walked aimlessly along the Boards, I had to train myself into patience and hope that the life soon to be offered on the Boards would, like my future life, have some quality, some excitement which would make it worth waiting for.

10

Hello Happiness, Farewell Honesty

In my new home in Logan, I went to the local state school. A year later I was sent to Akiba Hebrew Academy. This was a different world. Jewish but different. Here I met prosperous Jewish children, sons and daughters of lawyers, doctors, bra manufacturers, herring distributors, shop keepers who wanted their children to have a modern yet at the same time, a Hebrew education. These were children whose homes had games tables, sophisticated musical equipment and grand pianos. Now as a scholarship child, I had a different and strange feeling: I was an outsider among Jews. Even the Jewish instruction was different. Hebrew classes were conducted in modern Hebrew, not in Yiddish or singsong Ashkenazi. My horizons widened. There was a Jewish culture and civilization beyond my own – that of *mitzvot* and the *Talmud*. There were also Jews who did not worry about what they ate, did not pray regularly and still felt Jewish. I had to learn that my Jewishness was not the only way. This gave me a sense of uncertainty in my only area of security and so decreased my self-confidence.

Ironically, therefore, in moving from a non-Jewish school to a Jewish school, I exchanged one set of identity problems for another. In one I was a minority because I was a Jew, in the other because I was poor and orthodox.

I entered the Akiba Hebrew Academy at age of eleven in the sixth grade. It was an extraordinary change. In my public schools I was one of forty children sitting in rows behind solid desks. In Miss Fisher's class, there were only about a dozen of us and we sat in a circle. It was as though I had rejoined nursery school. I had become a person again.

Learning was not by rote. Not only did Akiba teach Hebrew in two forty-five minute sessions, one in Bible and one in Modern Hebrew, but it was also a progressive school inspired by a professor of education at Temple University who believed that formal learning should be integrated with a project relevant to the child's experience. So, one year, our task was to build a house. We divided into groups, each having its architect, builder and interior designer. Mathematics, design, home economics and study of building materials were all involved as we drew the house, laid its foundation stone, built its rooms and decorated them.

The following year we built a city. This involved a study of the geography and climate of the U.S.A., and debates on where our model city should be located. What was the ideal spot? We researched Fresno and Santa Barbara, California; Phoenix, Arizona; Salt Lake City, Utah and other sun drenched cities to make the decision. We studied city government and learnt about the various ways a city could be governed. Was it to be a Mayor or a City Manager? Once we decided, our class became the City Council. Committees were established to plan the city's shape, the street names, the number of houses, schools and parks. It was all great fun. It taught us how to relate to others. Even the class cynics could not help but be sucked into the projects. It was a wonderful theory but could work only up to the seventh grade, because then we had to get down to meeting the exam standards by which we would be judged worthy to enter college, not to mention the qualifications required for Medical or Law Schools.

The teachers were inspired by the concept. Only a few stayed for longer than two years because this fledgling school, it was only in its third year when I joined, could not offer its teachers the security provided by the state system. They were dedicated and were full of interesting ideas. One teacher had us listen to classical music and write an essay on the scene or story we thought it was portraying.

The teachers had lively personalities. One was very stern

but absolutely fair. He had a way of making you want to meet his standards. Another had invented a brick which was double sized in length. After school he rushed to the factory financed by his father-in-law to supervise their manufacture. It was his view that larger bricks could cut down the cost of labour in building a house. But would not larger bricks break more easily? Would they not be more difficult to lay? Would they make as nice a pattern? And would brick layers want to save the cost of their labour? And if they did not, could they not sabotage our teacher's plan? This was the debate among twelve year olds. Most of us didn't think it could work, and that he would lose his father-in-law's money, but as he had taken us into his confidence, we kept this to ourselves. Why hurt his feelings or dash his hopes?

The impact of Akiba on me was enormous. It became a home away from home. Akiba helped me develop my relational skills. My intellect and sensitivity were not taken for granted, as was the case at home. I was praised. I was encouraged to stretch myself. I felt that the teachers loved me. I am not so sure that they really did, but when a teacher looks you warmly in the eyes and smiles and says, 'I liked that Sidney', is that not as close to love as most people ever get. I cannot be sure, but it is possible that I evoked a special sort of sympathy because I did not come from the prosperous Jewish middle classes. While I never felt it, the teachers must have known that I was there on a scholarship and that I was different. But in fairness all the children who responded to their interest received the same caring attention.

Surely no smile, no word of praise, no wink of affection given by teachers to children is ever wasted. They are as real as a birthday present or a ride in Disneyworld. I still remember those signs of concern and affection. They nourished me and made me feel that the world was good. There are many mothers and fathers who, due to their own emotional turmoil or work pressures, are unable or unwilling, or too ignorant to meet their children's needs. These are parents who only notice their children when they are causing trouble. While teachers may spend less time with a child than his parents, their impact can be far greater. There can be an intensity in a moment's grace that can carry you through a lifetime if it tells you that you are important and deserving of love. There was a Hasidic rabbi who taught that one should become an atheist when you are approached for help, Why? Because if there is *no* God only *you* can help. This is the way teachers ought to be. Blessed are the good teachers because their children inherit a better world.

It was also not until I went to Akiba that I experienced group dynamics. While I excelled in certain areas of school life, I was weak in others. I learnt that others could take immense pleasure out of things which meant nothing to me and that each person saw what he excelled in as particularly relevant. Popularity resulted from doing well in those areas which the majority of students felt were of higher priority in their scale of values.

For the life of me, I could not understand why the girls went mad over basketball. Herschel Sklaroff was a god at Akiba because he could get the ball in the basket with more frequency than any other student. He was good looking too. That must have given him the confidence to dribble the ball quickly down the court before popping it into the net. While I was bemused by the excitement over a basketball game with a rival school, I had to accept that for many life could revolve around a ball, especially when they were good at knowing what to do with it.

But it was not only basketball. There were the chess players, and there was the school newspaper, of which I eventually became the Editor. There were also circles of interest which centred around certain children, who by their force of personality, developed into ring-leaders. Somehow, by being their friend, you achieved status. I never knew why I never joined a clique or wanted to become the centre of one. In spite of my increased socialization, I still was essentially a loner. I was never good at small talk. Even today I am amazed at conversations of children and adults which go nowhere.

For me, everything had to have a purpose. I guess that is
what we mean by a serious child. The ring leaders were great
conversationalists. They gossiped. They mixed it. They
praised and maligned. They made life less boring by embel-
lishing it, by asking hypothetical questions which had the
affect of enlivening conversation. It went something like:

> 'Do you think Joan likes Harold?'
> 'No, how could she, he's in love with Carol.'
> 'So what, she could still like him.'
> 'I know, but he's not her type.'
> 'I saw her looking at him the other day.'
> 'She looks at everybody.'
> 'Let's ask her.'
> 'You ask her.'

When I overheard conversations such as these, I could not
believe my ears. These conversations take place in all schools
and by both sexes. But it was my first experience of it. Such
directionless talk was never heard in my home, and when on
occasion it was, I remember my father saying disapprov-
ingly, *'veibishe reden'*, wives talk. I did not want to be an
intellectual snob. It was my upbringing. The Zaydeh, the
arbiter of values, condemned gossip as one of the cardinal
sins. Frivolous talk led to evil deeds. One of the worse sins
was *Lashon Hara*, evil language. By this, my Zaydeh did not
mean expletives or curse words. These were words I was
never to hear until I went to Yeshiva High School. *Lashon
Hara* was simply gossip. In this category, he even included
speaking *good* about people. 'Shimshon', he would say to me,
'When people say nice things about others, you can be sure
that eventually they will say, 'but' and then go on to say *not*
such nice things. That's why the 'wise men', may their
memories be for blessing, said that it is better to say nothing'. With this moral training, it was not natural for me to
engage in such talk. I had no conversation, unless I had a
question which needed a real answer or I had an idea which I

wanted to share. Thus kids only spoke to me when they
also had an objective for their conversation, because otherwise they received a 'I dunno', which they interpreted quite
correctly as 'nor do I care'. I must have been a bore.

I suffer from this prejudice until this very day. I *now*
realise that words can *also* be a form of stroking, of affirmation; that some people, particularly in country areas, resent
conversations which are too direct. Even when they have a
purpose, they walk around it several times before they
approach it. For many, talk is an affirmation of existence. I
was brought up in the tradition of 'cogito, ergo sum', assert-
ing my humanity by thinking. I have changed over the years,
though I still feel resentment welling up in me during meaningless chatter. I have tried to accept conversation as an
important way for bonding relationships. All the same, my
mind often reverts to the story told of Bernard Shaw.
Returning from a dinner one evening, he was asked, 'Did
you enjoy yourself?' He responded, 'There was no one else
to enjoy'.

All in all, the first few years in Akiba gave me many happy
days. They enabled me to extend myself beyond my family.
My world was enlarged and for the most part pleasantly.
There was, however, one experience in my first year at Akiba
which stands out in sharp and unpleasant contrast to all
others. It was unexpected and therefore all the more painful in that environment. I felt akin to the child who is told to
jump, does so in trust and finds that there is no one there
to catch him.

I never was a goody goody, but Akiba had made me feel a
sense of loyalty. The teachers were warm and loving to me
and it was natural for me to reciprocate. Perhaps, for that
reason and the general innocence of childhood, I showed an
error in judgement which was to cause me confusion and
bring me undeserved disapproval. It happened this way. I
had to telephone home. I went into the 'phone box, inserted
my dime and couldn't get through. I pulled the refund
plunger and out came a load of change. I collected it and

walked to the secretary on the office below and returned the money. When I told my class mates what had happened, they looked at me dumbfounded. They laughed at me, 'The secretary will keep it. Do you think she's going to give it to the Bell Telephone company?' To my recollection, there was no teacher who came to my defence. Indeed, it is possible that one teacher confirmed the cynical view. When I returned home to seek approval for my moral action, my parents also smiled as if to say, 'He's only a child, he will learn'. That was a moral lesson that I am afraid I have never forgotten, and I attribute a lot of the moral confusion in my life, my uncertainty about what is right and wrong to that incident as well as that of my mother changing price tags on two ties. In a world where a child's goodness wins no prizes, even at such a wonderful school as Akiba Hebrew Academy, is it any wonder that integrity is at such a premium?

Foretaste of the World to Come

The real beginning of my decision to leave home and go to boarding school at Yeshiva High School in New York City, must have been when Milly walked into my life. She was my older brother's girl-friend and they were to be married. Romance and excitement entered my life with her. My 'mythical' brother, because I rarely saw him before then, became a reality to me because of his relationship. The quips and glances they exchanged, their teasing and banter, their shared sexuality brought life, otherwise absent, into our house when they were visiting.

Milly took me by storm. My life had been one of getting centre stage only by demanding attention. She hurled it upon me. She showed up one evening, 'So you're Sidney, come let's take a walk'. There I was walking with this total stranger. 'I'll teach you a game. It is called to the crack and back, you walk to the last crack in the pavement and then you walk back'. How was one to cope with such dynamism, a girl who made walking into a ridiculous game? But I was entranced by the effort she was making to make me her friend. My brother's girl-friend wanted me to be her friend. For the first time in my life I felt needed.

I admired her expressiveness. 'Your brother is such a bastard', she said to me one morning, 'He wouldn't sleep with me'. This was said with no anger and appeared to be one more way that she sought to make me part of her experience. Milly lived a life with missionary zeal. Her objective was to teach me that life was good, that nature was beautiful, that books enhanced life and basically that it was up to each of us to make the world into a wedding. From my Zaydeh, I learnt

the pleasure of the use of the intellect, and from my older
brother, Chanan, the joy of reading. Though I did not see
much of him, whenever he came he always brought a book,
*Little Lord Fauntleroy, Toby Tyler at the Circus, The Wizard
of Oz, Dr Dolittle*. I identified with the characters and my life
was enlarged, as I experienced joys, anguish and pain at a safe
distance.

But Milly taught me, or tried to teach me, that all was possible, that I was not a captive in the world in which I was
born, that the only restrictions in life were those you imposed
upon yourself by not having the gumption to break through.
For her, life was a combination of heroism and optimism.
Every person could be a conquering hero. There was no trace
of romanticism in her pragmatic philosophy of life, because
romance was tied in with fantasy and the tragedy of spurned
love or unobtainable goals. Disappointment in life or mis-
chance was to be seen not as a defeat but as an opportunity
to ascend to greater heights, to prove oneself worthy and to
make one's success more fulfilling and enjoyable. When I
later studied Talmud, I came across the rabbi who, whenever
misfortune hit him or his community, would respond, *'Gam
Zoo Latovah'*, this too is for good. This was Milly's philosophy. There were no disadvantages. If she liked you, you
were special, and your weaknesses could be converted to
strengths, and proper use of your strength could make you
even more special.

My eldest brother was a truth teller, the more unpalatable
the truth, the more he loved revealing it. No one was spared.
The more he loved you, the more truthful he felt he had to
be. Milly was different. She was the arbiter of truth, and
chose the truths by which she and those she loved could best
live by. Chanan took the world for what it was and his only
criticism was for those who blinded themselves to the face of
reality and who lived lives of hypocrisy and self-delusion.

Milly was a relativist only in the sense that she determined
which truths could help her lead her life as an heroic opti-
mist. Like William James in *The Will to Believe*, she believed

that she could create truth by faith. An impossible chasm between two cliffs could be crossed if you believed you could do it. In her own life she proved this by never accepting defeat and never wearying of the task of converting failure into success. She chose her truths, and once she chose them, they became absolute for her. The way she was to raise her daughter, suffering from brain damage during childbirth, confirmed to me her god-like qualities. Under Milly's tutelage her daughter was to develop, marry and have three children. The Rabbis say, 'He who saves one life saves a world'. I saw Milly save one world and help create three more by the power of her faith and the determination of her will. She was to prove to me that all was, indeed, possible.

In my case, she decided that I was a person with talents and perception. I was worthy of cultivation. She would open up to me the world of natural beauty and human art. Flowers and plants took on meaning for me as she gave them names, and expressed her appreciation of their colours and shape. She read to me Oscar Wilde's *The Happy Prince* – the beautiful tale of the protected prince who only learnt of suffering after death, became more sublime because of the love with which she read it and the knowledge that she wanted to share its loveliness with me.

The wedding took place in a cool autumn evening in her mother's back yard under a *Chupah*, a canopy symbolising the nuptial chamber. It was a small wedding. The younger children seemed to be enjoying themselves more than the others for whom the wedding appeared to be a formality to which their attendance had been required as a sign of family unity. My brother wore a *kittel*, a white gown signifying the purity and sanctity of the occasion. Because he was no longer orthodox and this I was not to discover until later, he wore a raincoat to hide the *kittel*. Milly wore a white dress. To keep her mother happy, [her father had died when she was a child] she followed the orthodox custom of walking around my brother seven times. This was to indicate that, as his wife, she would be his protective wall. In truth it was the drawing of a magic circle to put off the evil demons who seek to spoil happy events. The Zaydeh addressed the wedding assembly and spoke glowingly of the aristocratic rabbinic ancestry of my brother, comparing it to the richest cream of Jewish society. Following his address Milly overheard her mother say to the Zaydeh, 'Reb Frankel, you should know that my family was not skimmed milk'.

Sometime, after their wedding, I was invited to visit them for a week. I don't think my mother wanted me to go. She was afraid that Milly would become the other woman in my life. She was prevailed upon and I went, and got my first glimpse of intellectual radicalism. I was usually in the company of my brother, as Milly was working. I heard Chanan talk of Stalinists and Trotskyites. I was shown Union Square and told of the war of trade unionists against the capitalists. I visited the apartment of a budding economist where there was no surface uncovered by books, magazines and papers. This was the period when Stalin's barbarism was coming to light, and I was fascinated to hear the discussion of present and former yeshiva students applying their Talmudic reasoning to rationalising Stalin's behaviour or condemning it. There was great passion in the discussions and they made me believe that they believed that their conclusions could make a great difference to the future of the world.

Although I did not appreciate it then, it was from that period on that I realised the influence of Talmudic study on the development of Jewish boys. Whether or not they forsook the study of Judaism, the imprint of Talmudic logic and argument always remained with them. A passion for systems of thought and complete clarity of thinking was their hallmark. Whatever emotional prejudices they had were rationalised into one system which in their eyes was as clear as transparent glass. Any view which did not fit in was derisory. When this view came from an individual who was accepted as being bright, it was either seen as an unfortunate blind spot or due to a malicious streak. One can well imagine therefore, the obsessional passion with which debates took place and

still do between Jews with this kind of Scholastic background.

What was not fun for me during this visit was the painful
discovery that my brother was not orthodox. I felt repeated
pain every time he flicked on the electric lights on the
Sabbath. I felt confusion each time he explained why he was
breaking a Jewish law. He coupled logical reasonableness
with warm tolerance. He was not going to prevent me from
being as orthodox as I liked during my visit. What he did not
realise was that he was putting me through hell. Here was my
role model in conflict with my normal life pattern. What was
I to do? The fear of God, the belief in the inviolability of
Jewish tradition, the conviction that what made me different
and better than others was my adherence to Jewish rituals,
were being assaulted by my older brother. My soul became
a battle ground. Like Jacob on the other side of the brook, I
had to wrestle with an angel. Was I to hold fast to the faith of
my childhood bolstered by the traditions of centuries,
attested to by the genius of my Zaydeh and the loyalty of
my father, or was I to cut the umbilical cord and go free into
the wide world, supported only by the knowledge that my
brother had also cut the cord and appeared to have survived.
At that time, I did not think in these terms and as I write, I
feel pompous in attributing such importance to the turmoil
in the life of a child. What did it all matter? It mattered a
lot. Henry V, before the battle of Agincourt, is aware that
the peasant soldier, contemplating the consequences of the
oncoming battle is no less involved in his destiny than the
king is in his.

I maintained my orthodoxy, but the seeds of confusion had
been sown in me. I had lost my resolve. My love for my
brother required the same tolerance towards his ideas as he
had shown mine. My acceptance of his integrity weakened
the ideological shield of steel which could have protected
me from future internal doubts and external assaults. I had
become vulnerable.

I recall being in the kitchen of my brother's squalid flat.

We were sitting around a rectangular table. It was in the days when margarine had been introduced. The butter lobby was fighting the margarine lobby and had won a battle. Margarine was not permitted to look like butter for that would confuse the innocent purchaser, and so inside each cellophane wrapped pound of margarine was a separate clot of colour substance to make it seem like butter. My brother was kneading the bag to spread the colouring throughout the margarine to make it look more edible. This image has stuck in my mind. Perhaps my recollection has a metaphorical basis. Had I, little Sidney, hard as clay in my orthodoxy become malleable like the margarine, and would I take on the colours kneaded into me by the influence around me, to which, since that historic visit, I was no longer impervious.

12

God in his House

As the ethnic nature of neighbourhoods change, it is a common occurrence for churches and schools to be converted into synagogues and for synagogues to become mosques and Sikh temples. Throughout my childhood days, however, the three synagogues my father attended were all converted private houses.

The first was on 7th Street in North Philadelphia. To call it a townhouse would suggest a grandeur it did not have. It was an attached house, the width of which could not have been more than twelve feet. There were two or three stories. The ground floor, originally two rooms, had been joined into one for the sanctuary. The floor above was used for the *kid-dush*, the name for the blessing over wine, which was also the term for refreshments after services. The length of the prayer hall was no more than thirty feet. Along part of a side wall, there was a cupboard for the *sifre Torah*, the scrolls of the Mosaic law, in front of which was a red velvet curtain embroidered in gold thread with the Lions of Judah. A large wooden lectern from which the Torah was read stood near the Ark. Some straight-backed chairs and benches lined the other walls for the worshippers. There was seating for no more than thirty men and I never recall seeing a woman in the congregation.

The contrast between that little dingy house of worship, in a declining section of Philadelphia and the stories I had heard of Solomon's Temple in Jerusalem impressed upon me the decline in Israel's majesty and grandeur over the centuries. It revealed the truth of the words prayed by Jews over the centuries, as the Torah is returned to the Ark, 'Bring us near unto you and we will return. Renew our days as of old'. I felt the presence of God less in his house than in my own. This was not surprising. I wouldn't want to live there, why should he?

The name of the synagogue was *Machzikay Hadas*, the Strengtheners of the Faith. It had no rabbi and my father would often lead the services. There would be constant mumbling of Hebrew words, interspersed with the leader singing the last sentence of a paragraph, to give the congregation an idea where they were at and the opportunity to say, Amen. There is an historical reason for the mumbling of the prayers. In life, there exists the need to expand. The more space, the more clutter; the longer a history, the greater the burden of tradition. It is easier to collect than to throw away. The Jewish prayer book was victim to this process of uncontrolled expansion. Over the course of centuries, Jewish religious geniuses had written poems and prayers and later they had been included in the liturgy. At other times, men of authority had decided that certain sections of sacred literature were too important to be omitted from the prayer book. Thus, in over two thousand years, Jewish prayers, which once had been simple, sharp and to the point, expanded to the point that if one wished to say the entire morning service sincerely and properly, it could take two hours. It has always been a mystery to me why orthodox Jews have not heeded the Mosaic command not to add or subtract from the law. True, orthodoxy has never subtracted but they certainly have added. The result is that a simple religion has been converted into a complicated series of instructions and restrictions, many appearing meaningless to ordinary human beings.

But back to the point; limitation of time and the determination of Jews to say it all meant that the prayers had to be recited at a gallop. This would have been easier had it been acceptable to read silently without the moving of the lips. But it was Jewish tradition that because a barren Hannah moved her lips as she prayed to have a son, all sincere petitions had to be made with moving lips. The quick movement of the lips causes a murmuring. When Jews pray with feeling, the murmur becomes a mumble. When ten Jews or more pray together, each has still enough individuality to want to hear his own mumble. It is not a soothing sound, because as no two people laugh or snore alike, no two Jews mumble alike, nor have they learnt to mumble together in harmony. So as a child all I heard in synagogue was a cacophony of meaningless mumbling.

Also because God was prepared to save the cities of Sodom and Gomorra if ten righteous men could be found, ten men were considered to constitute a Community for the purpose of collective worship. This was the *minyan,* the count. A mourner could only say *kaddish,* the prayer sanctifying God's power, in the presence of a community. As he was obligated to do this during daily prayers of the year of bereavement, it was necessary to gather a *minyan* and that is why we sometimes hear of the search for the Tenth Man. It was sad when a mourner would come to pray and there were only six men present. The men would identify totally with the mourner, because there was that sense that someday it could be them who needed to say *kaddish.* There was also the superstitious feeling that the dead were helped, slept more peacefully, perhaps, if the *kaddish* was said, not only during the first year, but on all subsequent anniversaries of his death. Not to give the mourner the opportunity to say *kaddish* was not only to let him down but to let the dead down as well.

Heads huddled together to weigh up the likelihood of finding the needed individuals. It reminded me of neighbourhood gangs trying to get two sides together for a softball game. Depending on the mood of the group, or the persistence of the mourner, the game would be given up for lost or search parties sent out to collect more individuals. With each additional worshipper found, the tension rose as the stakes got higher. By the time nine was reached, there was the sense of being very close, but yet so far. The search for the Tenth Man appeared as important as finding a crock of gold at the end of a rainbow. The tension increased as those Jews who

had been persuaded to come to make up the *minyan* waited to
see whether there had been any purpose in being dragged to
synagogue, because without the Tenth Man, their presence
was useless.

I remember when I was about twelve years old, being at
the *shul* of the Tolner Rebbeh. With great effort, eight men
had been found to meet a rich mourner's desire to say *kaddish*
one Sunday evening. I was present with my father who had
responded to a phone call for help. We only lived around the
corner. It was a great disadvantage to live so close to *shul*.
You were like a doctor, always on call. The nine men were
desperate. Only one more was required and not a male Jew
over thirteen to be found. The Tolner Rebbeh could lose a
big donation if the Tenth Man could not be found for the
kaddish to be said.

I do not know whether it was a case of necessity being the
mother of invention, or if the sight of the possible donation
blinded all other considerations, or if there really was such a
tradition but suddenly I heard the elders speaking in soft
tones to the *rebbeh*. After leaving some time for silent reflection to add weight to their decision, I heard that worship
would be possible. The solution had been found: in times
of emergency, when a Tenth Man was lacking, if a boy
approaching Bar Mitzvah held a *Tannach*, a Jewish Bible,
that act would add months or years to his age and he could
become the Tenth Man. So it was, Bible-in-hand, I shot into
adulthood and enabled some poor rich Jew to say *kaddish* for
his dad.

During the High Holydays, we went to stay with the
Manistrichter Rebbeh. His home was a mansion in comparison to our flat. The living room, which he had converted into
the synagogue, was large and actually looked like a place of
worship. There was an elevated platform for the reading of
the Torah in the centre, with pews behind it and on both
sides. In front was the Holy Ark. It was simple but dignified.
The *rebbeh* also gave the synagogue a feeling of importance.
There I felt that, even if I was not struck by the holiness of

God's presence, his representative at least was putting on a good show on his behalf. It was only right in my child's mind that God would dwell in a nicer house on Rosh Hashanah and Yom Kippur because the New Year and Day of Atonement were the holiest days, and if not then, when?

God seemed to come up in the world as the Brichto family did. When we moved from our two bedroomed third floor flat to a proper, though attached house in Logan, the synagogue we attended was also, although still a converted house, more substantial. It was a well-built and luxurious corner home. The dining room adjoined the living room, which was the synagogue proper. This opened into a sun room, which was used as the *rebbeh*'s family room during the year but was converted into a hall for overflow services during the Festivals. On these occasions all the furniture was removed and wooden folding chairs, lined up in rows, took their place. The seats in the sun room were cheaper than those in the main synagogue.

The dining room was used as the women's section. A few ladies which included the *rebbetsin* sat silently around the table and looked into their prayer books. On Friday evenings and Saturday mornings, services would take place in the synagogue. On weekday mornings and evenings and on Saturday evening, services would be held on the ground floor, which also had a reading desk and a small ark containing one scroll. It was to this lower floor, that the congregation retired for refreshments: the blessing over wine and bread, the drinking of *schnapps* and the eating of cake and herring, whenever the occasion warranted it. Following every Sabbath morning service, there was a *kiddush*. If there happened to be a Bar Mitzvah or an *Oof-roof*, when the bridegroom was called up to recite blessings over the scroll on the Sabbath before his wedding or a child-naming, the *kiddush* would be more elaborate as the celebrant, in addition to a donation to the *rebbeh*, would provide the drink and food.

Downstairs was where we had the *shaloshidis*, a Yiddish corruption of the two Hebrew words, *shalosh seudot*, meaning three feasts. It was obligatory for Jews to celebrate the Sabbath with three meals: Friday night, following the Service, Saturday noon and one more. The final one, known as *sholoshidis* took place between the *minha*, afternoon service, and *maariv*, the evening service, which concluded the Sabbath. As there was no time for a proper meal, and as the worshippers could not be expected to go home between the two services, the *rebbeh*, in his munificence, provided portions of *gefilte fish* which he himself sliced and passed down to his disciples. *Gefilte fish* is chopped fish usually made from Pike, Bream, White fish or a mixture of them. Ceremoniously, he cut the fish, for not only was he enabling his guests to fulfil the *mitzvah* of eating three meals, but he was dispensing his grace by sharing his food with them. This custom was called *schreiim*. It harked back to the times when the Hasidim believed that their rabbis were Holy Men. There are some who still believe this of their *rebbehs* to this day: notably the Lubavitch and Satmar sects. They would eat the remains of their food in the belief that it could bestow mystical powers on them. In our family we had no such feeling for the Tolner Rebbeh. He came from a family of *rebbehs* – the Twersky family – many who, like the Tolner, had set up shop for themselves. He had performed no miracles, nor had he brilliant aphorisms or great scholarship to his credit. As far as my father was concerned, what he did provide was a nice *haymish*, a homely shul, and that was enough.

During *sholoshidis*, we would sing Hasidic *nigunim*, tunes without words. Every once in a while someone would introduce a new *niggun*, which he had picked up somewhere. A *niggun* was considered a success if the tempo could be increased, with growing enthusiasm to the point that everyone was lost in the magic of the tune. Occasionally the *rebbeh* would provide an insight into some scriptural text or Hasidic saying. This did not happen too often, and I do not recall any of them ever making any impression upon me.

What I do remember with fondness is standing by him,

this man with a thick black beard covering a gentle and uncomplicated face, while he recited the *havdalah*, the blessing over wine, spices and candle light which concludes the Sabbath. *Havdalah* in Hebrew means 'distinction' because these final blessings praised God for separating the holy from the profane, light from darkness and the Sabbath from the six days of the week. After the Tolner Rebbeh drank the wine, he would spill some out into a saucer, dip the six-wick candle in the wine and extinguish it. He would then dip both his little fingers into the wine, touch the sides of his eyes and then, repeating the dipping several times, touch his earlobes, his groins, and finally his pockets. The Abah explained the reason. The *rebbeh* did this to improve his eyesight, his hearing, his potency and his wealth.

The Tolner Rebbeh's *shul* was informal and cosy. The *rebbeh* would sit in a chair in the corner which had a lectern in front of it which enabled him to rest his prayer book, when sitting or standing. On the Sabbath there would not be more than twenty-five present who would mill around the synagogue, sitting or standing as they liked. Although the Sabbath morning services began at nine, it did not matter what time I arrived, so long as I did not embarrass my father by coming disgracefully late. During the readings from the Torah and the Prophets which would last for forty minutes, it was normal for the younger people to go into the Sun Room with their printed Torah texts, which they could follow or hold on their laps while they chatted on every subject under the sun, with the exception of the biblical readings. I was the youngest and I learnt a lot about sex while pretending not to listen. As I grew older and was bored by the repetitiveness of worship, I would often, even on Friday night, go into the Sun Room where the prayers could still be heard, sit down on the sofa and set myself the productive task of memorising verses from the Psalms or Song of Songs which were part of the prayer book.

Even in the main synagogue, there was a lot of chatting going on during the prayers. This may have been God's

house, but in defence of our disrespect, was he not our father
and should we not relax in our father's house? There were
times when a visiting preacher expressed shock at the noise
and lack of respect in the *shul*. He would shout '*Mawkom
kodesh*', [this is a] holy place' several times until everyone was
quiet. The *rebbeh* being of a generous spirit allowed him to
ascend to the platform, to give us hell for our lack of respect
to the Almighty. We would listen politely but as soon as
he left, make fun of him, shouting at each other, '*Mawkom
kodesh, mawkom kodesh*'. The prigs in the congregation,
however, would say, 'he is right you know, he is right', but
continued talking all the same.

The *rebbeh* never preached. Indeed, unless there was an
appeal for funds, there was no sermon during Services. It was
a great thrill for me when the Zaydeh became our neighbour
in Logan because he was invited to preach on the only two
occasions that the very orthodox are prepared to tolerate
sermons: *Shabbat shuvah*, the Sabbath of repentance, which
falls between the Jewish New Year and the Day of Atonement and *Shabbat hagadol*, the 'great' Sabbath before
Passover. It was a remarkable performance. The address
would begin at about three. He spoke for two hours without a
note. He started with a biblical verse, asked a question about
its meaning and then unwove a Talmudic spider's web of
arguments, thrust and counterthrust, point and counter-
point, becoming ever more intricate and complicated. At the
very last minute he returned by some nifty foot work, like a
spider back into the centre of the web, and then back to the
starting point of the web, namely the original verse, which by
this time had been forgotten, to resolve by his new interpretation all the problems he had raised. Congratulatory shouts
of *sh'co-ach, sh'co-ach*, more strength to your elbow, were
hurled at him as they rushed to shake his hand for his *tour de
force*. I was very proud that he was my Zaydeh.

The informality of the *shul* was accentuated by the fact
that it was the *rebbeh*'s business and livelihood. The *shul* was
like his shop and God and Judaism were his stock in trade,

invisible but there all the same. This was very obvious because following each *aliyah*, a person being called to the Torah, and there were no less than eight such individuals given this honour on Shabbat, they was asked whether they wanted a blessing. If the answer was yes, they had the opportunity in the middle of the blessing, to tell the Reader who chanted the scroll reading, how much they wanted to donate to the *rebbeh*. I remember my father refusing an *aliyah* because he felt that he had given the *rebbeh* sufficient financial support that month.

On Festivals, the commercial element became fascinating because they auctioned off the *aliyot*. To be called up third or sixth as well as last, which gave you the right to sing the prophetical reading, was considered more prestigious and therefore fetched higher prices. It was amazing. I would hear the auctioneer shouting, 'two dollars for the third *aliyah*', and then he looked around for a higher bid and so it would progress. Sometimes, when the price soared, we looked for the rich stranger who had come to show off his wealth. We all knew that the money went to the *rebbeh*, but somehow it did not appear crass or mercenary. After all, there were overheads, and the *rebbeh* had to live and had a family to support. What was really fun was when they auctioned off the right to buy the *rebbeh* the honour of *his* going up to the Torah. Here one was paying the *rebbeh* so that he would not have to pay himself to have an *aliyah*. 'Who will give ten dollars for the *rebbeh* to have the sixth aliyah?' We would wait in suspense. Had the bid been pitched too high? Would the *rebbeh* be embarrassed if the price were lowered to five dollars? We all sighed with relief when a customer was found and the *rebbeh*'s face was saved. He would look around to see if there were any higher bids before closing by mentioning the name of the generous donor.

As is apparent, God's presence was not very noticeable in the Tolner Rebbeh's house either. There was no grandeur which could be identified with the thunderous God of Sinai, nor was there the silence of God as heard by Elijah, nor the moral inspiration as echoed by the other prophets. But while we did not feel his presence, what we did experience was constant evidence of his long standing relationship with our ancestors which we had inherited and were still determined to keep alive.

The non-evident God in this house was also fun loving, and there was no better illustration of this than the celebration of *Simchat Torah*, the festival of the 'Rejoicing in the Torah'. During this festival, the young people went mad and the adults with spark followed suit. It was extraordinary. On the night of the festival, the build-up of excitement was palpable. All the chairs and benches were removed from around the platform to make room for the parading of the scrolls.

At about nine, by which time all had assembled, the scrolls were taken out of the ark. There were five or six in addition to the miniature scroll, ten inches high, which was held by the *rebbeh*. All were hand written on parchment skin, each involving a year's labour. The scrolls were handed to leading members for the first procession. The *rebbeh* would be at the head of the procession, holding the Torah by the two wooden poles around which the parchment was rolled. In a sing song voice, the *rebbeh* would chant the prayer, 'It has been proven so that you may know that the Lord is God, there is none beside him'. Thus, the paeans of God's praise began. Everyone joined in. Children marched carrying flags decorated with pictures of the Ten Commandments, drawings of lions which were the symbols of the tribe of Judah, and its most notable descendent King David. Silver crowns were on the top of the scrolls. Apples were stuck to the top of the flagsticks and often lit candles would be placed on the centre of the apples, adding danger as well as romance to the festivities. After circling the platform, there would be singing and dancing in front of the Ark accompanied by Hasidic songs. The verses were from Psalms or medieval poetry. There was great competition each year to come up with a new song and chorus. The singing was frenetic. The object was to stretch your vocal chords to breaking point, to work yourself into a sweat. I remember my joy when my Abah had learnt a wonderful acrostic song in Brooklyn, praising God, Moses and Torah in successive letters of the Hebrew alphabet. It was sung nasally because it was an oriental composition. Everyone joined in the chorus and agreed that it was a smash hit.

By the time I was twelve, I was the only child of that age who was a regular at the Tolner's. I had joined an orthodox Zionist youth group led by several teenagers of the congregation and there were a number of boys and girls of about my age who came to my synagogue to see the *rebbeh* dance. Because my father was an influential member, I could be sure that as the scrolls were transferred from one group to another, my father would eventually get a scroll into my arms. I would lug it around the *shul*, leaning against my shoulder, my father behind me to give it additional support just in case. As we marched around, the scrolls would be kissed or people would stretch out to touch the Torah mantle and then kiss the fingers which had thus been sanctified. As I held the Torah I would be wished long life and many other blessings.

The sight of the *rebbeh* doing his shuffling dance and the men dancing around, scrolls in hand are a vivid memory. Why were we so excited? I guess it was because we wanted to be excited. The Torah was all that we Jews had and we were determined to go into ecstasy over it. Seven times the scrolls and flags paraded around the synagogue and seven times there was dancing in front of the ark. When the celebration was over in the synagogue, the younger people would move to the streets and dance the *hora* and other Israeli folk dances until they were ready to collapse. Since the Jews had by force of arms established the State of Israel, there was a resurgence of confidence which made us feel able to express our Judaism without shame, even in the Christian streets of Logan. When I came home perspiring and with a hoarse throat, my mother warned me that I would become ill if I carried on this way.

Would the mother of a non-Jewish child had complained if
her son had come home sweaty after playing hard to win a
football game. Along with fasting on the Day of Atonement,
Simchat Torah was the way I proved my Jewish maleness by
going into a frenzy over the Torah.

The fun continued into the morning of *Simhat Torah*. The
scrolls were paraded once again for seven times before the
last portion of Deuteronomy, the fifth book of Moses, and
the first portion of Genesis, were read which indicated that
the study of Torah never ceases. For some reasons pranks
were encouraged. While the men were immersed in prayer
or reading the Torah, we boys would untie their shoelaces
and tie one shoe to another. We would give 'hot foots', that
is placing the head of a paper match between the sole and
the upper shoe, then lighting it and waiting for it to reach
the head and burst into flame. Strangely enough, it was
permitted to light fires on Festivals (excluding the Day of
Atonement) unless they fell on the Sabbath. Now, I am
convinced that the older men knew what we were doing but
pretended innocence in order to give us more pleasure.
Sometimes things got out of hand, when a few of the older
boys started shooting seltzer water at each other, and the
rebbetsin was not pleased as she saw her home being flooded.

Where was God in all this? I do not know, but I felt that he
approved. As for my Zaydeh, he had too much dignity and
inhibitions to dance with the madness of the others but he
smiled wistfully and even approvingly, because he was grateful that we were loving our Jewish heritage. Perhaps, this was
also God's attitude: aloof but pleased that we were still wor-
shipping him and rejoicing in his Torah with such carefree
abandonment, in spite of the suffering and destruction that
had been the Jewish experience for millennia.

I used to visit a neighbouring Conservative synagogue
when their late Friday night services did not conflict with
services at the Tolner's. There was a rabbi and cantor at the
front of the synagogue on a platform. There was no central
platform. All the action, the scroll reading and the sermons

took place there. Indeed it reminded me of a theatre. No one talked during services and men and women sat together. The sermon was in English, not Yiddish, and was an essential part of each service. We orthodox lads went both to mock this 'goyish' form of Judaism and to drink tea and eat biscuits at the *Oneg Shabbat*, Delight of the Sabbath, reception following the service in the Assembly Hall. We looked for faults in the rabbi's sermon, and took delight in his love of superfluous repetition: 'And they gauged out Samson's eyes, he was blind, he could not see'. There was great dignity, but it was not 'Jewish'.

When I was to go to Rabbinical College, Henry Slonimsky would teach me of the three manifestations of God: The *Ein Sof*, the Infinite who was the God of mystery, the *Elohim*, the God of Power who was the cause of the natural wonders of creation and *Adonai*, the Lord, the Holy-One-Blessed-be-He, who was the God of goodness, and who wants to be the father and king of all of us, but we reject him, and so we suffer. Slonimsky felt that the God we related to was the Holy-One-Blessed-be-He. We argued with him as a rebellious child does with his father and we criticised him as suffering subjects do their king. I must have been captivated by this view because this is the way God appeared to me in my own upbringing. He could not be so august or so powerful; otherwise, he would have looked after us better. He was like us and we were like him. We were struggling with him to make a better world and we were thrilled because he had chosen us to be his partners in this great moral enterprise.

Eva, Marchioness of Reading, in her autobiography, wrote of her conversion to Judaism. She did this out of loyalty to her Jewish forbears and as a moral challenge to the Nazis who included her name on their hit list when they invaded Britain. She reminisces how on one Yom Kippur, in the North London synagogue where she was converted, she heard the rain beating down on the corrugated metal roof and she thought to herself, 'And for this I gave up Westminster

Abbey?' At many times in their history Jews gave up the Jewish God for One with greater power. The fact that so many did not, is why every *Simhat Torah*, there are still so many Jews dancing with scrolls and waiting for the day when the whole world would dance with their God.

13

It's his Money, let him spend it the way he wants

One thing I could have done without was a Bar Mitzvah, but the year 5722 according to the Jewish reckoning had arrived and during that year on the second day of the month of *Av*, I was to reach my thirteenth birthday, become a Jewish man, and assume full moral responsibility for my actions. On that day my father would say, in Hebrew, of course, 'Blessed be he who has freed me from this moral responsibility'.

Because I was my Zaydeh's grandson and the Abah's son, I had to do more than most boys who, on the designated Sabbath close to their Jewish birthday, would chant a few verses from the Torah reading and about 20-30 verses from a prophetical reading. I, however, had to learn to sing the whole Torah reading of a hundred and twenty one verses in addition to the prophetical reading.

It was put to me by my father in the most seductive terms. '*Shimshon, es is a groyser kovod zu zein Bar Mitzvah in Shabbos Nahamu*', it is a great honour to be Bar Mitzvah on the Sabbath of Consolation. You see, I was born exactly a week before the anniversary of the greatest national catastrophe in the Jewish People's calendar, [this was of course before the Holocaust] namely, the destruction of the Second Temple by the Romans in 70 C.E. On the Sabbath following the Ninth day of *Av*, the day of the Temple's fall, Isaiah Chapter 40 is the prophetic reading. The chapter begins: 'Comfort ye Comfort ye my people, says the Lord'. What follows are the most beautiful verses imaginable. Their resonance has been given further glory by the music of Handel's

Messiah. I am still thrilled when the contralto sings, 'O Thou who tellest good tidings to Zion' and am transformed by a vision of a better world when the tenor sings of the day when 'Every valley shall be lifted up and every mountain and hill made low'? The Torah portion of that Sabbath also includes the 'Ten Commandments' and 'Hear O Israel, the Lord our God the Lord is One', the verse which has been the declaration and rallying cry of every Jew and the words on the dying breath of every Jewish martyr.

'All very nice', I thought, but the preparation would entail a lot of hard work, which could only deflect me from what had become the great passion of my life, to give my newly-born niece all the love and affection which I myself had missed. Of course, I did not know my subconscious need for all the kisses I gave Judy and for all the embraces and for all the songs I sang to her. I justified my overwhelming love on the basis that neither her mother, my sister Ruth nor her husband nor the two grandmothers knew how to raise her as well as I could.

Every time Judy cried, I ran to her bedroom to take her out of the cot to cuddle her. 'Sidney, leave her alone' was the cry from my sister. 'A child has to cry. She will go to sleep soon'. When I was prevented from rescuing Judy, I would wait for five minutes and appeal, 'Something must be bothering her, can I pick her up now?' Not yet, Sidney'. And then every minute, 'Now?' If Judy stopped crying, I was disappointed both because I could not go to her and had to listen to my brother-in-law crowing, 'You see Sidney, a baby has to cry'.

Thinking about in retrospect, I must have driven Ruth and Norbert, her husband, crazy by my interventions and know-it-all attitude. My sister Ruth certainly did not deserve such treatment. She was a very loving mother. She was jolly and gave me the little physical affection I enjoyed during my childhood. Many years later she confessed that on the day of my marriage she had decided to have another child, to replace the baby she had lost in me. She conceived her third child on my wedding night. Norbert was less than twenty-two years old when Judy was born and Ruth was about nine months older than he. If Norbert hated me I could not blame him. How could he know, if I didn't, that by showering affection upon that child, I was really loving an extension of myself. My passion for Judy was irrational and my anger, when I was thwarted in giving her the attention I wanted to give her, was akin to that of a lover's jealousy.

Stendhal said that falling in love was loving a projection of oneself. My own experience has taught me that the euphoria of love is based on an egocentricism which only appears to be centred on another person. The courting lover who cannot be too protective or do too much for his beloved suddenly turns cold and finds his beloved too demanding after marriage, because, once married, he who was babying himself by babying another now wants to be babied himself.

I certainly was loving myself by loving Judy. You may ask how was it possible for me always to be so near to hear Judy's cries? Since my sister Ruth lived next-door in an attached house, I could hear the crying through the walls. It was a mistake for my sister to move next door, and I knew it. Selfishness, however, won the day. When the proposal was made for the young couple to buy the house I did not protest at this violation of my sister's marriage and privacy. Indeed I am not sure that I didn't even support the crazy proposal that a hole should be made through the cupboard wall under the staircase in our house which would join the cupboard under Ruth's staircase. The reason for this proposal would be to give us intercommunicating homes so that we would not have to go outside to visit each other. Somehow, sanity prevailed, probably on the basis that there would be no room for coats or galoshes if the cupboards were made into a hall or that it would detract from the market value of the houses; and not because the idea was totally mad.

When Ruth and Norbert went out for the evening, I baby-sat for them. They were grateful as was I because then I had complete control. I went into Judy's room and sang her all the folksongs I knew: *Black is the Colour, When I was a Bachelor, I Gave my Love a Cherry and On Top of Old Smokey* and *Three Brothers in Merry Scotland*. I also sang to her, *Me and My Teddy Bear* which had just become a hit and as I sang, 'Have no worries, have no cares', it was the truth during those happy moments of undemanding and requited love.

The preparation for my Bar Mitzvah would rob me of time to spend with Judy. But I made the best of it. Weather permitting, I would sit on the three-seater sofa glider on our porch. Judy would sit on my lap with a cushion against the arm to support her back. She would glide with me as I rehearsed the singing of my Torah portion. This is the strongest memory of my Bar Mitzvah period, gliding slowly on balmy spring and humid summer days, monotonously chanting the verses, on occasion breaking off to smile at Judy and readjust her on my lap.

After hours, days, weeks and months of preparation, I finally mastered the texts and the musical notes. I was relieved because there was still a month to go before the event, which would be in the middle of August. I could now enjoy the rest of the summer.

So I thought, until I was summoned to my grandfather's study, a five minute walk from my home. My grey-bearded Zaydeh was sitting at his desk and in front of him was his Hebrew typewriter. He said to me in the kindest voice, 'Shimshon you know it used to be customary for a boy on his Bar Mitzvah to show a bit of learning by explaining a *din*, a law. It doesn't happen now because the boys today are *am ha-ratzim*, ignoramuses, and do it for the presents; but *you* are different. Would you not like to make your Bar Mitzvah special by giving a *derasha*, an exegetical sermon?'

I thought to myself, 'That's what I'm looking forward to – the presents', but what I said, after taking a deep breath was, 'Zaydeh I would like nothing better, but what could I teach?' His response was immediate, 'Don't worry, so long as you want to do it'. With that reassurance, he pulled out from the

typewriter a sheet of paper, put it under two other sheets of
typewritten Hebrew, connected it with a clip, handed it to
me as though it were a present and said: 'You see, here it is, I
have done it for you', and there in unvocalised Hebrew, on
two and a half sides of paper, was the detailed explanation of
why, on the Sabbath, Jewish men do not wear *tfillin*, the
black boxes with scriptural verses which are bound to the
forehead and the top of the left arm, as they do during morning prayers on weekdays. I gulped, gratefully took the papers
from him and spent the next month memorising and telling
Judy why, had she been a boy, she would not have to wear
tfillin on the Sabbath. I had to memorise the speech because
reading it would not give the same ring of authenticity.
When you did it by heart, it appeared as if you really knew
what you were talking about.

The big day came. At last, seven men were called up to
the Torah and each in turn recited the blessings before and
after I read a section. The congregation rose to their feet
when I chanted the 'Ten Commandments'. I said the blessings over the Torah, which praised God for having chosen
us from among all peoples by giving us his Torah, and
implanting within us eternal life, sang the last few verses of
the Torah reading, before the recitation of the blessings over
the prophetical reading and the singing of Isaiah chapter 40.
As I sang these verses, I knew that there was still a Hebrew
disquisition to deliver.

When I completed my *derasha*, shouts of *Mazel Tov*,
good luck, and *sh'co-ach* were heard throughout the tiny
synagogue. I looked sheepishly at my Zaydeh and Abah and
quietly apologised to them for leaving out a key paragraph in
the speech, without which the explanation of why we don't
put on *tfillin* made absolutely no sense. My father smiled and
using a Talmudic phrase said, '*My nafke meena*, what difference does it make? Only the Zaydeh and I noticed'. My
relief that I had not let the side down was qualified by the
teeniest bit of resentment. 'Hell, if no one understood
Hebrew, why had I spent so much time learning it'. When at

the reception at our home the next day, a relation who could not attend the Service said, 'I heard you gave a wonderful speech. I'll give you another dollar if you do it again', I said, 'No thank you'. I blocked the speech out of my consciousness the moment the last syllable left my mouth. I felt that I had lost enough integrity by giving it the first time.

In addition to the fountain pens, wallets and other paraphernalia Bar Mitzvah boys collected in those days, I received $220, and within a day had decided to squander it all on a gigantic 12" television set, which the entire family could enjoy. My parents did not resist and my brother Zvi and Ruth and Norbert, who came in from next-door to watch were pleased at the communal feeling which motivated me. If my parents had had any moral stamina they would have vetoed my decision. They made some weak protest. 'Couldn't you find something better to spend your money on?' 'It's his money, let him spend it the way he wants', was the view of my siblings. The idea that it was a waste of time to watch television was weakened by the fact that I had first watched television at the home of none other than the Tolner *rebbeh*, the very Hasidic Rabbi who owned the house-synagogue at which I prayed and at which I was Bar Mitzvah.

I think it was in 1948 that I wangled an invitation to see the Milton Berle Variety Show on T.V. It was just before 8:00pm that I rushed through the dark streets to the Tolner *rebbeh*'s living room to see the magic of people thousands of miles away appearing right next to me. As Hasidic rabbis were supposed to be capable of performing small miracles for their Hassidim, it was quite fitting that it should have been the Tolner *rebbeh* who was the first to bring the magic of T.V. into the Orthodox circle in my neighbourhood. When we remonstrated that what was good for the Tolner should be good enough for us, my father was too respectful to indicate his low regard for the man's scholarship or priorities.

And so, just as Judy gave me pleasure before my Bar

Mitzvah, television was to add amusement to my life after-
wards. I would lose myself in laughter at the antics of Sid
Caesar and Imogene Coca, learn to appreciate the wry
humour of Jack Benny and Bob Hope. While T.V. may have
been a waste of time, it did enlarge my world. Certainly,
compared with the pleasure of loving Judy and watching
television, the preparation and performance of my Bar
Mitzvah came a poor third in the influence it had on the
development of my character.

14

To Read 'Sforim' or
Books is the Question!

My brother Chanan was giving himself a wet shave during one of his visits to Philadelphia. The bathroom was small and I stood by its open door in the narrow upstairs hall chatting to him. I was about fourteen and suffering the pains of adolescence. While I shared my unease with him, I simplified my condition by telling him that I was bored with life. His response was immediate. He washed the shaving foam and hair from his razor, looked at me and said, 'You should read'. Most young people would have expected advice on how to improve their social life, or hobbies and sports. Surprisingly enough, Chanan's advice seemed natural, and I asked him, 'What should I read?' He answered, 'Those books that others have read and stood the test of time, read the classics and you will never be bored'. He elaborated on the enjoyment of books and the excitement that one can find in histories, biographies and novels. He told me he had read Dostoyevsky's *The Brothers Karamazov* three times and had vowed to read it once a year because of its profundity.

I treated advice from Chanan as a command. As the Zaydeh was my Jewish role model, my older brother was my mediator and bridge to the non-Jewish world. He had left home to attend *yeshiva* University in New York City when I was only six. Before then, my recollection is not of him but of his reputation as a good student. Because of the admiration in which he was held, he was called *Brighto* in school.

Chanan's rare return home made him more special to me. He arrived like a demi-god. In my childish mind, he had

gone out into the wide world and had survived. There I was
still afraid to sleep in the dark, to stay in the house on my
own, a bag of insecurities and here was my brother sufficiently confident to leave home. His reports of his life
impressed me as would tales from outer space. Everything
he said became magnified in my child's mind. I believed it
when he told us that he had a friend in his dormitory who
could only be awakened by the rubbing together of two
knives. He told me that he was going to bring him to
Philadelphia to stay with us, and I waited with anticipation
for the arrival of this incredible man.

Indeed, all Chanan's friends had the aura of heroic crea-
tures. For me they were giants, first because they were bigger
than me, secondly because they arrived from outer space and
finally because I could not understand what they were saying
even though they spoke English. They spoke of politics and
economics, of countries and individuals with such intensity
that I assumed that their knowledge was first hand. I could
not know that it was only theory. It was natural, therefore,
for Chanan to become my point of reference for information
of the Western World. When at sea, captains of ships look
at the stars to see where they are. When I wanted to vent-
ure outside my family or my Jewish experience, I looked
to Chanan.

The day after he left, I took myself off to a book store. I
felt like Eliezer, Abraham's trusted servant, who was sent to
Padan Aram to bring back a wife for his master's son, without
a clue as how to meet this responsibility. What book should I
buy to start my reading project. It could not be the *Brothers
Karamazov*, that would have to wait. Chanan said so. There
were so many great books, how to choose one? Eliezer found
the solution almost immediately. God was on his side. He
was also on mine, because, in looking through the paper-
backs, I saw a book entitled *The Hundred Greatest Books*. I
turned its pages. It was all there neatly divided into sections,
the Ancients, the Greeks, Romans, Middle Ages, Modern,
French, Russian, English, American and so on. Each section

and book had a descriptive paragraph of fifteen to twenty-five
words. I had been given a structure for my reading. All I had
to do was to buy this paperback and then read the hundred
books. What could be simpler?

For a day I perused the book to see what was in store for
me. The next day, down to Philadelphia's most famous book-
shop, Leary's. It was a lovely place. It had three floors, and
next to it was a big covered alley, in which used books lined
two walls along its whole length. Buying a book was great
fun. The salesperson on each floor would write out the bill,
take your money, put it into a capsule, then into a tube and it
would shoot through the store and within a minute return
receipted with change. The hydraulic method of cash collection was once common, but Leary's book store was the only
one in my experience, and it gave book buying a magical
quality. There was also the pleasure of buying old books,
some over a hundred years old with inscriptions marking
birthdays and Christmases. To own a book published within
fifty years of the American Revolution made me feel that I
had bought a part of American history and made America
mine.

I loved buying books. In those days each book became a
friend. The cover was its face, the inside its personality. All
my money went on books, and as I returned from Leary's,
laden with books, my father would say: 'Why are you always
buying books? What are libraries for?' His attitude to the
books I read and purchased was an indication of the culture
gap which was growing between me and him.

The Abah *did* believe in buying books and paying good
money for them. But what he bought were not just books,
they were *Sforim*. Now, *Sforim* is the Hebrew word for
books, but a *sefer*, a single book, could never be a novel. It
was a book of Jewish learning. *Sforim* were the sacred texts,
commentaries on the sacred texts, the Talmud, the codes,
commentaries on the codes, legal responses, ethical teachings. These were reference books, not to be read but to be
studied and referred to throughout your life. How could

Madame Bovary by Flaubert or *Père Goriot* by Balzac or for that matter any 'goyish' history or biography compare? My books were for pleasure, an indulgence. His *Sforim* was learning, the essence of Jewish life.

In some sense my father's *Sforim* mentality was also part of me for I too purchased a book with the hope that it was to become a life long friend with a permanent place in my home. As Silas Marner collected gold coins because he had no other source of joy, no companions, little love, I collected books. In caring for them, and loving them, I was caring for myself, and I felt that I had achieved a relationship with the author which would not be possible if his book had to be returned to the library bookshelves where anyone could lay their hands on it.

I guess that my love for non-Jewish books was proof that I had become Americanised, that my Jewish background had ceased totally to envelop me. When I decided to read all the great classics rather than to spend my days memorising the Psalms of David, or learning each day a page of the Talmud, I was making a statement. It was not a conscious decision, and, had I turned to the Abah because of my 'boredom' and had he said, 'Shimshon, you should read every day this or that from Jewish literature', I might have done so and become equally excited about the possibility of mastering this project, as I was excited about meeting Chanan's challenge. Probably, my life would have been intellectually as rich, as was my Zaydeh's, though in a much narrower context, had I been motivated to master Jewish literature rather than the wealth of other cultures of the Western World and not just the one which was my birthright. Still, I did not turn to the Abah, nor to the Zaydeh, but to my older brother, and this indicated my own inclination as well as the charismatic power his personality had over me.

The Greek histories of Herodotus and Thucydides became the first book of my serious reading project. Over days, weeks and months I progressed to the Iliad and the Odyssey of Homer, the Greek tragedians and orators. On to the Roman period with the reading of Caesar's *Gaul*, the histories of Suetonius and Plutarchs Lives. The moral sense of the Greek authors impressed me, but I was shocked by the brutality attributed to the Roman Emperors and their families. The poetry of Catullus surprised me, as it was my first reading encounter with an author who described homo-sexual acts without condemnation. The discovery later that the Greeks were bisexual was to convince me that sexual attitudes were subject more to social mores than to absolute ethical standards.

I was reading at a feverish pitch, and particularly at the weekends when I could complete one or two 'heavy' books. For some reason I recall reading *Madame Bovary* one Friday night, finishing it bleary-eyed at three on Saturday morning. I recall the seduction of the heroine in the carriage as though I was there myself being carried through the streets of Rouen, and I recall the frustration of that unhappy woman, as though it had been my own. Stories of seduction, whether of Tolstoy's Anna Karenina or Hardy's Tess and Bathsheba filled me with ambivalence – sympathy for the women and envy for the men who could wield such mysterious power over them. My disciplined reading of the Greats began in 1950 and did not cease until 1955 when my reading lost its obsessive character and became more casual. My summer vacations were spent doing nothing but reading, so much so, that an old school friend still remembers how when he was looking for summer jobs to make some money, he asked me, 'Sidney, what are you doing this summer?' and my reply was, 'Reading'. He concludes the memory with, 'There was I *shvitzing*, sweating, as a busboy in the Catskills and Sidney, what was he doing? He was reading'. What my friend did not realise was that for me reading was work, though it was work I had chosen.

One major goal was to read my brother's favourite, *The Brothers Karamazov*, and in a sense I perceived all the books I read as training for the big fight, because Dostoevsky was a 'heavy' and his *Brothers* the heaviest of his punches.

Occasionally I would turn to the first few pages and have to confess, 'No, still too much to handle, I am not quite ready'. I could not yet cope with the myriad characters, each with three or four names, and details of the lives of each of the persona so easy to forget but so important to remember if later events were to make sense. When finally, at the age of seventeen, I read the book, I realised that the author tells his story as if he were telling it to a member of the family, and like any juicy titbit of family gossip, he expects it to be remembered without need for repetition. I learnt that that was the secret of enjoying any great novel: to plunge into it as though you were a relative of the characters keenly interested, if not passionately involved in the development of their lives.

Reading was not an escape for me from life. I did not read adventure books. It was the confrontation of life through the eyes and emotions of others, and it was of lives much richer and far more passionate than my own. The impact upon my character development was enormous. For example, while horrified by the greed and grasping nature of Balzac's creations, who would destroy others to enrich themselves, I had to accept that such people existed. And by the time I read *King Lear*, I could believe that there were daughters capable of such cruelty as Regan and Goneril. The wealth of characters and situations in my readings made me realise at an early age that no political or economic system could bring universal happiness. The world was about people, and the success of any system was dependent upon the individuals who led it. My belief that the highest value was the life and dignity of the individual and my contempt for any theory prepared to sacrifice individual lives for a 'common good' began at that time. Systems, like theories, could provide a structure but no more. When a government developed out of a gut struggle between opposing interests, there was more chance of it succeeding in providing its citizens with a better life, as was the case in Great Britain, than when reforming intellectuals exploit the oppressed to create a revolution, as was the case in the U.S.S.R. The best that one can hope for is a system of checks and balances which limits the powers of the rulers to exploit those they rule. These basic thoughts of mine, however they developed, found their source in the reading of fiction and history.

From every admired author I learnt something: the gentle cynicism of De Maupassant; the loving mockery of life by Trollope; the melancholy fatalism of Hardy; the freshness of George Eliot, and I could go on. Every author that I read during that period of my life can still arouse a mood in me, and has given my life a texture and richness. Modern authors have not been able to do this for me, and I can only attribute this to the fact that I read the Classics during my formative years, which gave them a special place. The only novelist that turned my head in later years was Hermann Hesse and, while I do not deprecate his work, I feel that my rapture at his writings was partially due to my own yearning for a return to youth with its promise of hope. Hesse seemed to say to me that all was possible and this is what I still wanted to believe as I passed the age of forty.

My reading was not an escape because I read in order to learn how people led their lives and the possibilities for living mine. It was not an escape, because it even reminded me of my own Jewishness. That was a surprise indeed, to see that Western Culture could not ignore the Jews. The antisemitism I encountered in literature, particularly from authors I admired was breathtaking. It was impossible, even if one wished to, to escape from one's Jewishness. The gentile world had made the Jews a multi-functional symbol. I enjoyed Charles Lamb's *Essays of Elia*, in spite of his criticism of Jews in 'Imperfect Sympathies'. I discovered different degrees of antisemitism, ranging from the relatively fashionable, harmless kind of the British aristocracy, to the violent hatred of the fascist poets. I was pleased to discover that George Eliot and Anthony Trollope liked Jews and wrote positively about them. I wrestled with the questions: could William Shakespeare be an antisemite because of his portrayal of Shylock and Charles Dickens because of his characterisation of Fagin? The constant allusions to Jews compelled me to question the role of the Jew in history and whether I wanted to carry on fulfilling this role. My extensive reading made me realise that while Jews might wish to isolate themselves from the non-Jewish World, it would not let them. They were a part of Western consciousness.

My absorption in the literature of the Western World, including the voracious reading of history and anthropology, made me look at my own religion more objectively. Were the traditions and beliefs of others only to be the subject of critical study and not my own? Was only my religion ordained by God? While these questions lurked inside me, it was safer not to answer them. Ironically, it was not long after reading Matthew Arnold's essay on Hebraism and Hellenism, that a wonderful line of Euripides was the fillip for my giving up orthodoxy. I wanted to mark it for future reference. Unfortunately it was the Sabbath on which writing, considered as work, was not permitted. I picked myself off the swing-sofa on the porch, went to my bedroom, found a pencil and underlined the sentence. Nothing happened. I decided to challenge the orthodox Jewish God and quickly switched on and off the bedroom light. No lightening struck me. The world had not changed by my acts, but my world had!

I wonder now what would have happened had my brother been a psychologist, who instead of advising me to read would have focused on my frustration as an ungainly adolescent. No doubt he would have advised me to start a programme of socialising. He would have taught me how to give up my inhibitions, so that instead of buying books I would have dated girls. If this had been so, what would have been the result? It is an idle speculation, but this was my fate. This was my background. Like it or not, for Jews of my ilk, life was first to be found in books, be they in the *Sforim* of my father or the used books on the shelves of Leary's. Perhaps I would have been a happier lad had this not been the case, but I feel that because it was, I became a worldlier and a happier man.

15

Flirting with Sigmund Freud

Puberty was not an easy period for me. I was told that George Orwell said that 'adolescence was like walking on a tightrope over a cesspool'. Whether he did or didn't, I kept falling in.

As I grew taller, I grew skinnier. My body did not fill out. My ears seemed to be making every effort to leave my face. I would stand before the mirrored medicine cabinet in the bathroom trying to push my ears closer to my face. I had worn glasses since I was eight years old. I was grateful for them now because I thought they made my nose look less like a skiing slope and were also a distraction from my ears.

While the other boys of my age were happily exploring their new-found sexual virility, I was totally unsuccessful in proving myself a man. It may have been the hernia which was the cause of my frustration or paralytic guilt, because Jewish boys did not do such things. The fact that all my friends who were Jewish did and talked about it depressed me further.

What was most embarrassing was that at about the age of about fourteen I began to have the most wonderful wet dreams, that is until I woke up in a situation which to say the least, was unpleasant. My mother who was meticulous also found it disturbing. I heard her ring up the doctor to find out what was wrong with me. He reassured her that I was quite normal. I was glad to have this confirmation of my virility, but unlike the other boys I had no control over it. The Censor, that clever creation of Freud who accounts for how the subconscious makes a fool of the conscious self, was able to hoodwink me every time. I could be having what appeared to be an innocent dream. All of a sudden I would be looking at a girl's downy leg and whoops! I tried sleeping on my side, but that didn't work.

It may have been the enrichment of my dream life which made me turn to Freud's *On the Interpretation of Dreams* for an explanation. Reading it opened up a Pandora's Box. I dreamed more than ever and *all* my dreams were crying out for interpretation. For example, I dreamt that I was overturning the earth in our back yard in order to plant some nice grass seed. In the dream my father is sternly rebuking me. 'Why', he asks, 'are you uprooting my garden?' Could there be any question about it? He was angry because I had begun to rebel against the Jewish tradition.

I dreamt that I lost my teeth, my hair and everything else that one could lose. I climbed up stairs, couldn't reach the top, fell down stairs, had all the dreams indicating fear of impotency and sexual non-fulfilment. I was living proof that Sigmund Freud was right! So fascinated was I by my discovery that I shared my wisdom with my classmates. I became, like Joseph, an interpreter of dreams. One day something really fantastic happened. A girl in class said to me during a break, 'Sidney, I dreamt that we were together in a field and there was a flower and I asked you to pluck it out for me, what does it mean?' Ye gods, I could not believe my ears. Was she having me on? Had she too read Freud? How could I tell her that on the basis of the wish-fulfilment theory and dream-symbolism, she was asking me to deflower her. I blushed, told her I was stumped, would have to do some research and would come back to her. Meanwhile, I decided that here was a girl I should sit next to in class and risk feeling up her legs under the table. But I did not because, being romantic, my heart was held in captivity by the unobtainable Ruthie Simon. More of her later!

That dream was the only positive outcome of my reading of Freud. I went from the Dream Theory to his other essays and became very introspective, reading myself and my

problems into every page of his analyses. I looked for the psy-
chosomatic reasons for my allergic asthma which occurred
during the hay fever season. Not being able to breathe was
bad enough. Looking for the emotional basis of my illness in
the hope that I could cure myself only made it worse. I now
felt responsible for my asthma because I did not have the
mental strength to overcome it. The increased tension made
my asthmatic attacks more severe, thus validating the psy-
chosomatic hypothesis which in turn increased my anxiety. I
was in a vicious cycle and regretted ever reading Freud. But
it was too late, I was hooked. I probed everything I did. I
realised that the scratching of my head and the collecting of
dry skin under my fingernails was a substitute for masturba-
tion. Did that discovery make me scratch less? No, it made
me scratch with even greater intensity.

No, it was not a good period. I had no one to see me
through this awkward stage of my life. Neither my father nor
mother had a clue as how to advise a self-conscious son on
how to walk along the tight rope of adolescence. My older
sister had married two years previously, had a baby and was
too busy facing the hard realities of marriage and mother-
hood to appreciate the problems I had and my need for
help. Because I was bright and doing well at school, it was
assumed that I was fine. My brother Zvi's emotional problems demanded all my parents' attention. They probably
would not have known of his suffering either had he been a
good student and suffered in silence.

I gave the impression that I preferred reading books to
'making out' with girls. Inside I was dying a hundred deaths,
wondering whether I would ever get my act together. I was
highly respected by my teachers for my precocious reading,
and my political skills in organising class council meetings.
At the age of fifteen, I read Orwell's 1984. My teacher asked
for my view of the book. When I said that Orwell had no
faith in mankind, he could not help but tell everyone of my
acute perception. I even managed to win the respect of my
classmates because I stood up for them in a crisis and was a

fairly interesting maverick: someone who read classics but was not a prig. But all this was little compensation for not feeling normal. Even though I was at a Jewish day school, I still felt like an outsider because of my poverty and Orthodox background. That, combined with my physical weediness and my struggle through puberty made my life a living hell.

All would have been well had Ruthie Simons loved me the way I loved her. She liked me but not with the same overwhelming need. The more secure and loving background which she enjoyed meant that there was not the same urgency which compelled me to develop our relationship into something warm and comforting. I needed her to fill the vacuum in my life. To her I was only one of many options for a relationship which, because of its short duration, could never be significant. Ruthie was what we used to describe as cute. She had a vivacious face with close-cropped black curly hair. The boys made fun of her piano legs, but I found her wonderful. She was lovely: neither fat nor thin; short nor tall. She was *zaftig*, the Jewish expression for cuddly. She and I were the two brightest in the class. Class politics and joint projects in our Progressive core curriculum kept us close. But she was rich. When she did not do well, or as well as she wanted to do in a subject, her parents gave her private lessons. She was also an American, by which I mean that her parents were born in the States. I did not have the confidence to pursue her. I did not dare to ask her out on a date because I did not know how to organise the journeys to and from her home in smart Germantown. School and parties to which we were both invited were the only opportunities for meeting. How to be alone with her on a school outing became the great challenge, at which I usually failed. At parties I was no use because I could not dance. I was too inhibited to throw myself around the dance floor. I had laboriously learnt the box step and was as square as the boxes I made on the dance floor and as wooden. I was hopeless. Not only did I not know what to do with my feet, I did not know what to do with my hands. In those days, you didn't dance cheek to cheek. There was always a distance between the dancing parties. You touched each other as you touch open wires, afraid that if you held the girl too firmly around the waist, you could be electrocuted. You talked as you danced but that too was difficult, in spite of my reputation as a good talker. I had to concentrate on not stepping on toes, saying sorry when I did, explaining away my lack of style, and waiting with desperation for the record to finish so that I could retreat to the drinks table.

The only way our relationship would have developed would have been for her to take the initiative; this she did not do, and why should she? At night I would try out my tele- pathic powers on her. If I could only make my thoughts hers! I would knit my brows, close my eyes and concentrate. I kept repeating, 'I love Sidney, I love Sidney'. The next morning in class I would wait to see whether my mental efforts had had any affect. They hadn't.

The approach of the vacations made me despair because this would mean that I would not see her until the resump- tion of school in seven weeks time. As the summer holiday approached, I would seek ways of establishing the contact which would open up the possibility of summer meetings, visits to the wonderful art museum along the Benjamin Franklin Parkway, followed by a picnic along the Schuylkill River. As the days became fewer, my desperation grew as I saw my hopes of success receding into nothingness.

The Spring of 1951 was a particularly bad one for me. I was agitated by my reading of Freud, a sense of failure and a loss of confidence. My mind which had always been my sole source of pride was also letting me down. I discovered that I was not adept at mathematics, languages or the sciences. I had to work hard on these subjects and the results were still not great. My talents shone in English and history. I began to doubt whether I could be the great success as a lawyer or doctor or whatever Jewish boys are good at. My body, which had never been a great morale booster also started crumbling. I discovered a rash in my right ear. I could not leave it alone and scabs developed. I removed them and back they came. I was really falling apart.

I felt I deserved a nervous breakdown. My problem was that proneness to mental instability was not my Achilles heel. My weakness was respiratory. I expressed my neuroses through asthma. This, however, did not deter me from enjoying a breakdown to which I felt entitled. My entitlement became even more clear to me when due to lack of determination on my part, or other reasons of which I was not aware, or which I have blocked, Ruthie was successfully wooed by others. In retrospect, this was to have been anticipated, particularly as the boyfriends came from the senior grades. This was no consolation as I was demoralized by the confidence with which older and more secure boys knew how to get what they wanted.

It was galling for me that one of my 'older' friends, Barry, perhaps not aware of the secret love kindling in my breast for Ruthie, succeeded in captivating her. With amazement, I appraised his approach. At first Ruthie didn't like him, but he threw himself at her feet. He overwhelmed her with sycophantic attention. It's hard to resist being loved with total passion. 'A fellow who loves me so much must have some good qualities', is the psychological reaction. Barry knew what I didn't and he was persistent. Once Barry won Ruthie's affection, he turned. He treated her like dirt. Barry's treatment of the girls he won by humiliating himself (and the revenge he took upon them for the necessity to do so to win their favours) became a byword among his friends: 'Ruthie, get your coat, we're going for a walk', was the command of her master. Ruthie would get her coat and they would go for a walk.

I laughed outwardly but wept inwardly, as even my fantasies lost any bit of reality needed to sustain them. My asthma increased. I could not sleep at night because of the wheezing and shortage of breath. In the morning I was too tired to go to school. For two weeks I languished at home.

Aimlessly and disconsolately I walked around the house. I read. I looked for things to do. I bought a two-ring binder and started a notebook. I filled it with self-analysis and quotations from famous men.

As an escape from my own frustrating life I read about the giants of modern history. I consumed biographies of Garibaldi and Cavour, Bismarck and Frederick the Great but especially Napoleon Bonaparte. He was my favourite. I regaled myself with stories of the miniscule Napoleon, who in spite of his size and his cowardice (it is not well known that in his initial struggle to gain control of France, Napoleon lost his nerve, was prepared to flee for his life and it was his brother Joseph who courageously saved the day for him) became a great conquering hero, bringing to his bed any woman he fancied. I loved the story told by Emil Ludvig of Napoleon sending for the famous actress, Mlle Duchesnois. He is busy working at his desk when he is told of her arrival. He tells the servant to show her to the bedroom. An hour later, the servant returns to say that the woman is waiting. He tells Constant, his servant, to tell her to take off her clothes. She is ushered into the First Consul's bedroom, undresses and gets into bed. Time passes until the dawn breaks. The servant comes in and tells Napoleon that the lady was still waiting. 'Tell her to go away', is the curt command. I wrote that story down in my note book. 'What power', I thought, 'and what style. Could that ever be me?' Well, it certainly wasn't going to happen to me in Philadelphia at the Akiba Hebrew Academy. If a change is better than a rest, it is certainly better than an induced nervous breakdown.

I recall watching Jews playing poker. One was losing and asked if he could change seats with his neighbour. As he made the request, he said in Hebrew: '*M'shaneh makom. m'shaneh mazol*', when one changes his place he changes his luck. That was my hope as I decided to leave my fifteen year old world behind me and seek better luck in a brand new world: the world of skyscrapers, of brownstone houses, of Broadway, Times Square and 42nd Street. The world of my brother Chanan beckoned me, although he at the time was serving as a Chaplain in Korea.

The only excuse I had for going to New York city was to deepen my Jewish knowledge at Yeshiva University's high school. The problem was that it was orthodox and I was not. I dissembled. With the help of my mother, my father was persuaded to let me leave home. Why she did not mind my leaving home, I will never understand. Perhaps, one less person to make a mess. He had his doubts about my motivation for going there. But he submitted to the pressure. The support of the Zaydeh was enlisted. He had gone to see Dr Samuel Belkin, President of the Yeshiva University to obtain entrance and a scholarship for my brother Chanan, and now he would intervene on my behalf. We travelled together on train and subway and were ushered into the President's splendid office. My grandfather spoke eloquently about my virtues, my determination, my love for learning. I was a good Jewish boy. Dr Belkin could not help but remind him of the desertion of my elder brother from the ranks of the pious, to which he replied with utter sincerity, making it all the more painful for me, as I squirmed in my seat: '*Shimshon is anandere shnit vare*', Shimshon is from another cut of cloth. I winced as I heard that unwitting falsehood leave his mouth. Fortunately, I was not called on to say anything so I was not required to lie. Due to the respect for my Zaydeh and his learning, I was accepted and given a scholarship providing me with room and board. On the train coming home, I felt some guilt for having used my grandfather to fulfil an ambition with which he would not have approved. The excitement of my new future, however, made it bearable. So, 'New York City, here I come.'

16

'I vunt to see your Mudder, your Fadder or vun of your Parents'

Whereas Akiba Hebrew Academy was warm and friendly, so was Talmudical Academy, the high school of Yeshiva University, cold, off putting and reactionary. It had a large student body and was the best compromise the neo-orthodox could make with the Western World. The whole morning was given over to Jewish studies and the entire afternoon to secular subjects. Those who did not wish to spend their entire morning in the study of Talmud were allowed a further compromise: they attended the Teachers Institute. Their morning was divided into a variety of Jewish subjects: Modern Hebrew, Jewish history, Bible, Hebrew literature as well as Talmud. Rabbinical students at Yeshiva College, in addition to their secular studies, only studied Talmud.

Learned Orthodox Jews only studied the Torah, – The Five Books of Moses – and other stories of the Bible when they were children. But every Sabbath, a section of the Torah was read, so that in the course of a year and every year ortho-dox Jews read it in its entirety. In addition, there were the Second Readings from the Prophetical writings, usually related in some tenuous fashion to the Torah reading. Also, the *Song of Songs* was read on Passover and by the pious, on every Friday evening. The *Book of Ruth* was read on *Shavuot*, Pentecost, and *Ecclesiastes* on *Sukkot*, Tabernacles; the *Book of Esther* during the festival of *Purim*, the Festival of Lots. *Lamentations* was read on the Fast of *Tisha B'av*, the 9th day of the month of Av, to commemorate the destruction of the Temple in Jerusalem. Psalms were an integral part of the

Jewish liturgy and the pious would 'say' the Psalms as Catholics say 'Hail Marys'. Other than that, all the other biblical passages were learnt when they were quoted in the Talmud to illustrate a point, or by the medieval biblical commentaries, to explain the meaning of one word or phrase by cross-referencing it with another. The greatest scholars of the People of the Book interestingly emphasize the study of the Talmud more than the Bible.

I chose to join the Teachers Institute because I thought it would be less demanding and also more interesting. Those who took the full Talmud option were considered to be the more serious students, and were therefore more respected by the authorities. They were the heavies. We, at Teachers Institute, were the dilettantes, and we were made to feel it, however subtly, by our teachers and the administration. It was *sina qua non* that if you wanted to sharpen your wits and be with the 'big boys', you had to study the Talmud. All other subjects were considered soft options.

While a student, the Yeshiva University was going through a transition phase. It had established the Stern College for Girls, indicating recognition by the neo-orthodox that girls too had the right to a university education. A Medical School was in the pipeline. The Law School, to my knowledge, had not yet been conceived. It would soon be possible for orthodox Jews to become doctors and lawyers at the same time that they were becoming Talmudists. What was to have been primarily a modern orthodox Rabbinical Seminary, was just about to take on wings when I entered its portals as an 11th Grade High School student.

From the start I was out of place, but I had anticipated that this would be my situation before my arrival. I was already non-orthodox and, therefore, attending on false pretences. I was prepared to play the hypocrite in order to get out into the wide world. The Talmudical Academy was my way for doing so. This was to be my adventure, the bridge between my dependent and independent self, and the chasm I would have to cross if I were to leave parochial Philadelphia for the Big

Apple of New York. What I did not anticipate was how different the environment would be from that of Akiba.

The school was cold and unfriendly for a number of reasons. It was very large with more than thirty in a class. Most of the teachers of the secular subjects were not orthodox and had no sympathy with the objectives of the administration. They found it difficult to relate to an educational philosophy for which their subjects were secondary to Jewish instruction, emphasized by the decision to give the most productive morning hours to Jewish study. For many of the teachers it was merely an opportunity for a second income because they could teach elsewhere in the morning. Also, there was no commitment by the administration to the value of a Western education. The value system being taught was based solely on Judaism and, therefore, the secular teachers had nothing to contribute. The objective of the administration was to prove to parents that their children could get a first-rate secular education and still learn the Talmud and other Jewish subjects. The only way of judging the achievement of this objective was through the results in the New York Board of Regents Examinations. This meant that the teachers taught the students for one purpose: to do as well as possible in these examinations. I grant that this probably was also the major concern at the state schools. This, however, added to the sense that Western education was viewed not as a storehouse of Western values but as a compromise with the Gentile world. This made the secular side of its education even more like a factory for producing good exam results.

Had the administration been friendly, it could have helped, but it was not. The high school, to my recollection, had no Principal. If it did, the man enjoyed a sinecure because he was never seen. The administrator was the Registrar, who also acted in this capacity in the Teachers Institute. His only role was to keep the boys in order. You only saw him when you were in trouble. He may have been a lovely guy but to us he looked and behaved like the governor of a prison. His name was Abrams; he had a heavy East European accent and our imitation of two of his quotations gives an indication of his relationship to the students. 'Chervin', he would say as he addressed one of his errant boys, 'I vunt to see your mudder, your fadder or vun of your parents' and this was still in the days when Jewish boys only had one set of parents. The other saying was when he questioned individuals who had taken off from one of their morning Jewish classes. (This was a paradox: while in the view of the administration these were the classes that mattered, in the eyes of the students motivated by the desire to do well in the state examinations, their achievement in the Hebrew subjects were of secondary importance – and for this reason there was far more playing hooky from these classes. Indeed, before the exam period there was wholesale cutting of these classes in order to cram up for the secular exams, or to catch up on some sleep as the result of sleepless nights of preparation.) Abrams would look at the student who had been sent to him by the teacher without a note of excuse for missing the previous class. He would ask in Hebrew: '*Kawtsastaw*', did you cut class. The student would come up with an explanation and then would hear the judgement, the one word in Hebrew, meaning 'You have justified yourself' or the two words meaning, 'You have not justified yourself'. Students who had gotten away with it would come out waving with joy the note of excuse from Abrams which would gain them readmission to class. The others came out with the knowledge that a note was to be sent home to their parents advising them of their behaviour and with the threat of suspension. That brings to mind another favourite quotation of his which had us students rocking with laughter: 'Freedman, you are suspended indefinitely for three days'. Abrams took great pride in the use of big English words, and who were we to deprive him of this small pleasure?

Adventurous kids stole the Registrar's excuse notebook and forged his signature after cutting classes. Because of the alienation between teachers and students and between the students and the administration, cheating was almost universal. Yeshiva High School was like an open prison. Of course, in all fairness I ought to say that in this it was no different from most schools orientated towards the passing of qualifying exams. The completion of the last exam in one's life must give the same sense of relief as a prisoner feels when his sentence is over. One of the greatest failures of Western Society is that it has not achieved an alternative state system of education to that which was introduced at the time of the Industrial Revolution. The massive weight of human frustration and the absence of moral values and purpose, other than success, is the consequence of modern man's failure to meet this challenge, while meeting so many others.

This promoted a sense of solidarity among the students who shared everything including answers to exams. The high motivation for success and good results led even the brightest and most studious not to refuse pre-knowledge of a test question or the opportunity to swap answers during exams. I remember only one of my classmates who refused to participate in such behaviour. Children being what they are, I thought it a credit to our class that on graduation they did not hold it against him; on the contrary, in recognition of his excellence in his studies and his school activities, voted him most likely to succeed, Best Personality and even Best Natured. Strangely, we respected him for his set of values but without feeling any guilt about our own lack of them.

The biggest joke was that because it was a Jewish school, Yeshiva University it was supposed to operate on an honour system which led one teacher to acknowledge the inner contradiction between ethics and reality by declaring before every exam, 'Lads, you know that we operate here on the 'honour system' and I intend to enforce it'.

Besides my secret non-orthodoxy, I had other disadvantages. I was a boarder while most students were day students. Most of the dormers were from one of the five boroughs of New York City, too distant for a daily journey but not too distant to prevent them from going home for the weekends.

This meant that I too returned home for the weekend and was excluded from sharing a social life with my dorm mates. Also, I had entered high school halfway through. My classmates had already forged their relationships, so I had some catching up to do.

As I could expect no teacher to take a personal interest in me, I had to make a go with the students. I remember the surprise of my English literature teacher when I seemed to enjoy reading *David Copperfield* which was required reading. He looked at me in pleasant disbelief. Once I came up to him after class to ask an intelligent question. 'Brichto, that's an interesting point you raise, I'll deal with it in class at our next session'. Whether he did or did not, I do not remember. He did smile at me during class and call on me to answer questions but that was the extent of our relationship. All the other classes were factual and allowed no opportunity for me to use my creative mind.

The student body was a very mixed bag. There were no entrance examinations. There were those who were bright and those who were limited. There were the studious and the slackers. All in all, they were a friendly lot. There was no expression of malice or viciousness between students. There were no bullies and even sympathy for those with limited intellectual capacity and it was considered right to help them out. There were some cliques but these arose out of shared interests and were never intended to exclude others. Those who had the capacity wanted to do well, but without that competitive spirit that is so common in English schools. A student who received 100% in an exam was very happy if his classmates received the same result. They were even kind to their teachers. I found them to be brighter, more fun and worldlier than my mates at Akiba. For the first time in my life, I encountered students who were more eloquent than myself. That was a salutary and necessary lesson for me and made me realise that my self confidence and security could not be based on the belief that I was the best in any area. There would always be someone able to do something better than me, and ultimately my happiness would depend on my being able to do the best that Sidney Brichto could do.

I don't know whether I learnt that lesson then, but it was the reason that the story of Reb Zusya struck such a chord in me when I first heard it. This Hasidic rebbeh of the town of Hanipol was lying on his death bed and weeping. When asked for the reason by his disciples, he replied, 'I know that when I come to the seat of judgement, I will not be asked: 'Why were you not like Abraham, the Patriarch or Moses the lawgiver', I will be asked why were you not like Reb Zusya, and that is why I weep'.

My fellow dormers and classmates kidded me about my Philadelphian accent, particularly the way I pronounced the letter 'O'; but that was the extent of the teasing, and as soon as I made the moves to enter into their activities, I was welcomed as a soldier in the army. I volunteered to be a Reporter for the *Academy News*, a two-page four-sided printed weekly journal. I decided to put my political skills to good use and my first article was an exposé of the authoritarian control of the high school dormitory. I called for a democratically elected dormitory council to have the power to govern themselves and to mediate their demands with the dormitory supervisor, a rabbi who appeared to be in training to succeed Mr Abrams. He looked like one of those customs officials at Moscow Airport, who never smile out of fear that such display of emotion is a betrayal of their sworn duty to protect their system.

Rabbi Feldblum had a nasty habit of opening dormitory doors with his pass key, without even a warning knock, hoping that he would catch a boy up to no good. This had to stop! Also, dormers had to register their attendance at the morning *Minyan*. It was a disgrace, I argued, that a yeshiva should have to monitor the praying of their students. Did this not imply that prayer is an unpleasant task and that we were not obeying the command 'to serve the Lord in gladness?' The editor read my article and said that Abrams would not let it pass. One member of the of the editorial board said, 'You forget, he can't read English'. 'Yeh', was the response, 'But when he hears what it said, he'll close the Academy News down'. 'Fantastic', I interjected, with visions of revolutionary excitement, 'We can then publish an underground newspaper. It will set the Yeshiva on fire and make us famous'. We published and were prepared to be damned. I gained enormous respect by that one effort, especially when I agreed to accept responsibility for it. I weighed up the risks of suspension against the potential fame and decided that I was in a no-lose situation.

The affects of my article were beyond my wildest expectations. The editor, Rosedeitcher, was called in to see Mr Abrams. He, by pre-arrangement, had argued the importance of a free press, that it was part of the American Constitution, and that he could not in all conscience prevent me from writing what I believed. He offered his resignation if he could not edit the TA News according to the highest standards set by the Declaration of Independence and the Founding Fathers. He indicated that there might be another editorial if no action was taken. Abrams was stymied. Rosedeitcher came out, smiled and said, 'Sidney, he wants to see you too'.

'Brichto, why do you want to make trouble?' I gave him a painful look. 'Sir', I said with the greatest respect, 'You do me a great injustice. I believed in what I wrote and I was certain that you would too, once the matter had been brought to your attention'. He looked at me. He seemed to be considering the options. What was going on in his mind, I do not know, but when he said, 'Next time come and see me, and whatever you think, don't dare print it. I will speak to Rabbi Feldblum'. I tasted victory in my mouth. We had won.

It was with great trepidation that I went to see Feldblum in his office the following day. The negotiations began. He agreed to the formation of a Dormitory Council and to knock twice before using the pass key. I had pressed hard for the right of total privacy, but the two knocks was a compromise and we had to let the dormitory council have something for which to fight. There was to be no register of minyan attendance but two students, nominated by the dorm council, would be responsible for assuring good attendance and reporting any individuals who were flagrant in their non-attendance. They never did and I was able to sleep later in the morning. I was elected as President of the dormitory council in recognition of my achievements. This established my position and compensated for the little pleasure I had in my classes. I did not have one teacher who inspired me.

I was surprised to find that I knew one of the teachers of Jewish history because for one year he had been the Principal of Akiba Hebrew Academy. He had not been very popular. He did not really believe in progressive education and by his leering look embarrassed the girls when they came into the Secretary's office adjoining his when they had an unanticipated menstrual period and required a kotex. At Yeshiva, however, he did give me some information which I found fascinating. He was the first to tell me that during the heyday of the Roman Empire, ten per cent of the population was Jewish, that there were Roman Legions which did not fight on the Sabbath because of their large number of Jewish soldiers. I was impressed to learn from him that when legislation touching the Jews came before the Roman Senate, one Senator implored his colleagues not to be influenced by their wives before coming to a decision. This was because their wives had converted to Judaism or were Jewish sympathisers.

This was to give me a much clearer perspective of the Jewish situation on the eve of the Roman conversion to Christianity. It made me appreciate the paradox of the transformation of the teachings of Jesus by the conversion of Paul. It is one of the great ironies of the history of religion that today Christianity is viewed as always having been a missionising and universal faith while Judaism particularistic and exclusive. Yet it was Jesus who, according to the gospels, attacked the Pharisees for crossing the seas to make one convert while neglecting the lost sheep of Israel. It was Jesus whose message was directed to his own people, and who said, 'Cast not your pearls before swine'. The realisation that Pauline Christianity had reaped the harvest that the Pharisees had sown, I owe to that history class. The realisation that Paul achieved this only by compromising with Roman Paganism was not to dawn upon me until later.

Other than that, there was a lot of scholarship and perspiration but no inspiration, and it was in school politics and in the antics of my schoolmates that I found my enjoyment. I took vicarious pleasure in the mischievousness of the more rowdy students, and this taught me that it was possible to sublimate through relationships one's own latent desires. A boy named Chervin became one of my closest friends. He would never study, got by on bluffing and double-talk. He would come to me in desperation and I would be pleased to help give him as much as I could. I would tell him what I thought would be asked in the exams. I would cram with him during all night sessions, even though he had little to give me in return. The day before one of the New York Regent's exams, he came up to me and confessed.

'I cannot pass. I need another week.'
'What are you going to do?', I asked.
'I dunno'.
'You'll have to pretend you're sick'.
'They will know I'm faking'.
'You'll have to vomit at the beginning of the exam'.
'How?'
'Drink a lot of carbonated soda at breakfast and eggs. When no one is looking, stick your forefinger as far down in your throat as you can. It can't fail'.

I never thought he had the guts to do it, but the next day at about 9:30 am I saw a pale faced Chervin sitting in the hallway outside the Principal's office waiting for a car to take him home.

The fact that the school was not co-educational, and

neither I nor the other boys were competing for the favours of girls, also helped. There was a camaraderie which would not have been possible were their girls to play up to. Without girls to distract me, without the emphasis on physical training and sport, where skill and brains and wit counted, I was in the right environment to see me through adolescence with minimal pain.

My proudest moment, next to my election as dormitory president was my role during Hobo Day. It was the tradition that each graduating class had to do something bizarre to outdo the shenanigans of the previous graduating class. In my second and final year, the class leaders came up with Hobo Day. On the appointed day, the day students kitted themselves out to look like bums. The appointed time came. The boys with torn jeans, sleeveless shirts, dirty scarves around their necks, green suspenders and frontless shoes nonchalantly walked into their classes after the opening bell. There was bedlam: all the kids were sent out to see Abrams. There was no room in his office, so they were gathered in the hallway. The teachers couldn't control their classes and many raised their hands for permission to go to the toilets to see what was happening.

A red-faced Abrams shouted, 'Boys, you are all suspended. Give your name to the secretary and go home'. Things had gone wrong. It was only a joke. The important mid-term examinations were in two weeks time. They could not afford suspension. Something would have to be done. A delegation was appointed to intercede on their behalf. I, who had not dressed as a hobo was chosen to be the head of the petitioners. There were three of us. We asked for an appointment to see Abrams. 'Vat do you vant?' he asked. I explained our mission. I pleaded with him. I told him that the boys meant no harm. They were following a tradition.

My speech had a Shakespearian ring to it. 'Sir, we come on behalf of our fellow classmates, to plead for them, their good name and the good name of the Talmudical Academy. We are fully aware that their manner of dress was not in keeping with the prescribed manner expected of T.A. Yeshiva students and caused disruption. But we ask you to reconsider whether the punishment you have meted out is merited by their misdemeanour. You, sir, must be aware that there is the tradition that each class must create a diversion during their year of graduation. True, they may have gone too far, but last year's class had set high standards which were difficult to surpass. And sir, consider the impact of so many boys being suspended. One boy yes, two boys maybe, even three, it is possible, but so many! What will parents think when they hear of the number? Will they not feel that the school is no longer under control? What is more, we are unable to guarantee that the rest of the class will not go out on sympathy strike. And you are aware that among the students you are suspending are some of the best in the class, boys who should be among your proudest graduates, perhaps the winners of school prizes.

'We come to you with a proposal. We will ask the perpetrators to dress properly and to give no further trouble.' He relented, saw our representatives, who were the three best students. 'Its all right, no suspension and back to classes on promise of good behaviour'. I became the hero of Hobo Day as we later celebrated with beers in the dormitory.

One day, a room-mate had been in a Jewish delicatessen; he had seen packets of beef frying. It was beef with a fatty trimming. Fried, it curled up to look like crisp bacon, and the burning fat made it even smell like bacon. This was too good to be true. My two room mates and I chipped in to buy some. We borrowed a frying pan and one evening started frying on our electric grill. We looked at the meat in amazement as the smoke and fragrance filled the room. We heard a knock on the door and then another. It could only be Feldblum. We were prepared. 'Come in!' we shouted. Nonchalantly we looked at Rabbi Feldblum as if wondering why he had come to see us. His face was red. His eyes looked as if they were going to pop out of his head. 'What are you doing?' were the words which fought to leave his mouth.

'Just cooking'.
'But what are you cooking?'
'It's obvious, meat'.
'But what kind of meat?'
'What do you mean? Meat meat'.
'But, but . . . !'

Abrams appeared to be gasping for breath to say the word, but it was hard for him to let it desecrate his lips. We were not going to help him. Finally, he whispered the word 'Bacon'. We looked at him and feigned utter horror. 'Bacon' we cried. 'Bacon', how could you suggest such a thing. We have never seen bacon in our lives, nor smelt it. This is beef'. We showed him the wrapping as evidence. There was a mixture of chagrin and relief on his face. Thank God we had not been guilty of the crime, but he had been humiliated. 'I am sorry but you must never fry this kind of beef in the room. It makes too much smoke, It looks like bacon and it makes the wrong impression'. We agreed but insisted that we be allowed to eat what we had already cooked, because it would be wrong to waste food'. Meekly, he nodded, turned and let himself out of our room. Our faces beamed with smiles. The beef looked terrible. We chucked it into a thick paper bag, tossed it into the bin, made ourselves some coffee and invited our friends to our room to tell them of our escapade.

During my stay in *yeshiva*, in this hotbed of orthodoxy, I never wavered in my heresy although, I tried to hide my true colours. I hoped to discover a kindred spirit but never did. Sometimes I skated on thin ice as I questioned the basis of many of the *mitzvot*, the commandments. For example, I pointed out the absurdity of the *shatnes* law. According to a Biblical command, one was not allowed to cross fertilise animals or to sow different seeds together. The command not to distort God's natural law, *shatnes*, made some theological sense, but one of its modern applications was the law against any mixture of cotton and wool. Once a year or so,

the *shatness* man would appear to investigate the boys' clothing, to see whether there was any such mixture present in
their clothing. The only place that this would occur is in the
lining behind the jacket lapels, intended to strengthen this
section to make it rest neatly on the shoulder. One kid was
very unlucky. *Shatnes* was found in his lapel. The *shatnes*
man hacked it out. The boy was incredulous, 'What will my
mother say? 'Tell her that Jews have suffered worse for their
religion' was his cold response. From that day on we agreed
to advise each other of his approach. The cry would go out
through the halls of Yeshiva University and High School,
'Beware the '*shatnes*' man is coming!'

When I developed my argument against ridiculous obser-
vances, my antagonists cried, 'Tradition!' and continued,
'Once you begin to give up some *mitzvot*, you end by giving
them all up, and that's the end of Judaism and we become
like the Christians'. I rejoined by declaring that it was
pathetic if intelligent Jews could not discriminate between
sensible and irrational commandments. Furthermore, obedi-
ence to ritual commandments cannot be the only thing that
distinguishes Jews from Christians. 'Is it possible', I asked
with as much scorn as I could muster, 'That Judaism has no
philosophy, no system of ethics which distinguish us from
others? Could our Judaism consist only in how we cover our
heads, wash our hands, what we eat and so on?' The power of
my arguments began to reach the authorities and I decided
for the sake of my Abah and Zaydeh, I had better shut up.

I graduated Talmudical Academy without much distinction; I had always perceived my two years there as a passing
phase. I was not geared up to making any permanent relationships. They were orthodox and still wedded to the world
I had left. My years at T.A. indicated that I could cope with
physical independence, and that I had the mental adapta-
bility to make any place my home, so long as I knew what I
was doing there.

17

My Beneficent Genie

One Saturday morning, in the Autumn of 1952, I left my dormitory to have lunch with Milly in her apartment at 181st Street overlooking the Hudson River. Her living-room window had a marvellous view of the George Washington Bridge, which spanned the states of New York and New Jersey. I remember with sad melancholy the times I spent there babysitting and there listening to Mozart's Clarinet Concerto K.622 while looking at the bridge and the occasional barges which passed under it.

Normally, I would return to Philadelphia for the weekend, but Milly had told me that the Dean would be coming to lunch, and a lunch with the Dean was too great an opportunity to miss. My brother Chanan and Milly had constantly spoken about him. He was Dr Henry Slonimsky, Dean Emeritus of the Jewish Institute of Religion, the rabbinical seminary which merged with the Hebrew Union College of Cincinnati. It was he who had made it possible for my sophisticated brother to consider the rabbinate as an intellectually acceptable profession. As Chanan and Milly were my role models, I anticipated with awe meeting theirs. I desperately wanted to make a good impression and nervously waited his arrival.

Chanan would not be present because he was still in Korea. Milly and I were speaking of him, when the bell rang and in walked the Dean carrying a bottle of wine, He was not handsome: age had taken its toll. There were bags under his eyes and his face was rather globular. His ears jutted out and were floppy. The face, however, was the screen for his intellect and passion. As soon as he spoke, it took on such dynamism that its physical qualities became bathed in spiritual beauty.

The mood of that Saturday afternoon remains one of those cherished recollections which gives me a contented feeling every time I evoke it. Bach's Suite No 1 and No 2 were playing on the record player as the Dean poured out the wine and Milly spooned out the eggs. The food and drink had the quality of nectar and ambrosia and I felt I was sitting among the gods and listening to the music of Apollo. The Dean was speculating on the nature of a man who could write such music. At one point he interrupted his flow to look at me and ask, 'Young Brichto, do you always eat *tarfut*, non-kosher food, wearing a *yarmelka*, a skullcap?' My Jewish readers, if they have gotten over the shock that I could have ever eaten *tarfut* will appreciate the humour. Covering one's head on all occasions is an act of piety among orthodox Jews and, due to my background, it was automatic for me to fetch a skull cap from my pocket and place it on my head the moment I went into a Jewish home; and this I had done even entering the liberated home of my sister-in-law. I don't remember my reply. I am sure I flushed and assume that we laughed together at the absurdity of the situation.

Life, however, is full of symbolism and metaphors and that event proved to be an indication of my future life. My *yarmelka* was a mark of my Judaism and my eating non-kosher food, or whatever else I did, would not, at least in my own perception, make me any less Jewish. The Dean had entered my life, and I chose to love him. I was well disposed to do so. As my own idols idealised him, my tendency was to worship him.

My Zaydeh had taught me that the intellect was the essence of human life. The objectives of the intellect, however, were narrowly defined. They were logically to determine God's will, based on certain assumptions and principles of induction and deduction. It was an exciting exercise if you enjoyed building a structure according to a blueprint and seeing a result which was faithful to the design. Because it was structured, the thought process lacked emotion.

But with the Dean, thinking was a robust exercise. His thoughts and concepts were expressed with such passion that they became a vital force. One idea did not need to lead to another. It could have a life of its own. Accordingly, you had to love the man, to enjoy the creativity which broke through all logical restrictions. His lectures were full of contradictions but this was a reflection of the nature of any human soul in conflict. Because Slonimsky was great, his inner conflict was greater. Those students who wanted neat packaging for ideas, theories which were totally consistent and capable of easy explanation did not respond to Slonimsky. He would make theologically shocking statements to his students, and then, as if reading their minds, say: 'Boys, you can't preach it'. One of my colleagues, who attended his lectures after I had been ordained, told me that the admission of women to the seminary had limited Slonimsky's style because he was too much of a gentleman to use the occasional expletive in their presence to emphasise a point. One woman student, who must have been driving him to distraction, chose to inform him that in his lecture he had contradicted a statement he had made in a previous session. She said this as she looked at her notes to indicate that she had the evidence. He looked at her and in repressed rage said, 'Miss Brown, you know what you can do with your contradictions, you can take them, put them into a milk bottle and send them to your *Booba,* grandmother. Just hearing of this incident makes me smile from ear to ear as I can see him say it, and know what he really wanted to say.

Slonimsky taught me that Judaism was not just the study of the past. Because Judaism belonged to the future, it believed in a Messianic Age and there was nothing good brave or beautiful in human life that could not be encompassed by it. He made me feel that it was possible to be a rabbi without surrendering one's intellectual integrity or one's lust for life or one's sense of humour. In his lectures there was the darkest realism combined with prophetic idealism. He would say, 'Boys' and this was the way he introduced all his lapidary utterances, thoughts which he considered worthy of being carved in stone. 'Boys, the Devil has been proved but not God!' 'Boys, the good suffer and the best suffer most'. But then he would say in the course of his lecture, 'In Judaism there is only one sin against the Holy Ghost [he had no reservations about using non-Jewish images if they served to dramatise a point] and that is despair'. He explained the essence of the moral genius. 'Boys, as the Romans tore the skin off Akiba's flesh and taunted the thousands of disciples who watched his agony by asking, 'Where is your God now?', Akiba in his dying breath said the Shema, the classic Jewish declaration of God's sovereignty, affirming that there was a God in a godless world'. Slonimsky telling this tale with the dramatic elongation of each vowel had the effect of convincing me that, Akiba by his affirmation had indeed imposed a God upon the world.

There was the curious mixture of humility and arrogance in Slonimsky's approach. He was in awe of the Greats of Jewish and human history. 'We must warm our hands at their fire' was the way he encouraged us to hold on to our faith. If such moral geniuses as Jeremiah and Isaiah believed in God, it should be good enough for us! Yet he was contemptuous of any Jewish thinker who did not agree with him and would be merciless in his condemnation. He saw them as pigmies in comparison to his own heroes. When referring to the thoughts of the founder of the Reconstructionist Movement, he would appear to be writhing in agony as he said that the man's face had been carved out of a turnip. What really angered him was not the man's face but his theology which had won the support of thousands of Jews, a theology which posited an impersonal God, the force for good. Slonimsky needed a living God, a God to struggle with, a God who was addressed as a lover, as a father, or as a king, not an abstract God who can only be addressed: To whom it may concern.

There was mystery in the universe which inspired awe and wonder, but this should not distract us from the importance of the human struggle for moral excellence. The mysticism which posits a pantheistic God, the Judaism which makes God the creator of evil as well as good, the fatalism in all religions which declare that *all* is due to providence was hateful to him. For Slonimsky, God *was* good but dependent on us for his power. He could only achieve his kingdom through his greatest creation, Man. As God had worked through nature to make the leap from monkey to *homo sapiens* and from the Stone Age Man to Jeremiah, someday, he believed, there would be another leap when all men would become moral supermen. Having declared that God could not act independently of humanity, Slonimsky was still full of irrational anger towards him for his impotence. Inconsistent, but no more than the ambivalence that a child feels for a parent who, much as he would like, cannot diminish his pain or fix his broken toy, or save his sick cat.

There was excitement in every encounter with the Dean and I looked forward to them in the way like to a lover's meeting. You never knew what stories he would tell, what reminiscences he would recall, and what insights he would reveal. You could always be sure, however, that you would experience the expression of passion, of love and hate in the most eloquent diction. Often when he wished to bestow special praise on a man, he would say, 'Boys, he was a great hater'.

At his lectures (which I attended for seven years during my undergraduate and postgraduate years) laboriously prepared in manuscript form, he would interrupt his theme to deliver unexpected home truths, such as, 'Boys only the happy can afford to be good.' Suddenly, with no reason, he would say: 'Genius has no morality but work. Lionel Barrymore would spend the night drinking and fornicating, but in the morning he was at the studio at work, the night as though it had never been'.

Because of his affection for my brother and sister-in-law,

we too developed a personal relationship. At the lunches at my brother's home, I would learn of the madness of the American fascist poet Ezra Pound and the disillusionment of the First World War English novelist, Richard Aldington both whom he knew and of other associates of his who became famous figures. On other social occasions we encouraged the Dean as our fountainhead of wisdom, to act as the Oracle and analyse the present company, to define their characters and to prophesy their future.

After lectures, I would often be invited to join Slonimsky for lunch at Horn and Hardarts at 72nd St and 7th Ave where we would eat pumpkin pie, which he, he declared, was the best in the world. On the way we would stop for a beer. The first time I had the privilege to join him, we stopped off at the first saloon; standing by the bar, he drank two thirds of the glass in one swallow. I knew then that this was not a social drink but a thirst-quenching stop on the way to meatier refreshment. It was at lunch that I would ask questions about his lectures, because in class I did not want to arrest the flow of his eloquence. He did not like to be interrupted, nor did he believe in class discussion. Occasionally he asked a question, but this was a Socratic device to achieve the answer he required. Once, I remember telling him what he wanted to hear in words almost his own. I remember his gratified smile as he looked at me and the class, beamed and said, 'My words come back to me with alienated majesty'.

Eventually, I learnt that this great man, so full of vitality, of mental energy, treated as a demi-god by many of his disciples was full of bitterness. He, in fact, considered himself a failure. He was in the ebb tide of his life, and he would have liked to have been able to bask in the fame and glory that was won by some of his associates. He had ended up in a back water, teaching rabbinic students, and while it was more than good enough for us, it was not good enough for him. In his own eyes he was a failure. He had never published a book, only articles which appeared in specialised Jewish annuals. It was said by some that his vanity made him fear the risk of criticism which greets every book and every new theory. It may have been his sense that he was only on the periphery of genius. However great he was to his students, compared to his heroes, he was a non-finisher in the race towards excellence. With ironic anger he would lift his fist to the class and say, 'Boys, it is a great scandal (elongated 'a' in the word scandal for greater emphasis) that we were not all born geniuses and beautiful'. Of course, I knew that he was not speaking of us but of himself. Genius had touched him like a strong wind, but he was *not* the wind.

For me, however, it did not matter that he was not a genius. He had changed my world. He made me confident that I could be Jewish and proud not only of Judaism's history but of its philosophy, that my Jewishness did not deny me the best of life but, on the contrary, it gave me the means to enrich it. When I read Deuteronomy Chapter 30; verse 19 on the morning of the Day of Atonement, it is Slonimsky I hear as I say the words, 'I have put before you life and death, good and evil, choose life and live!' His philosophy and passion had given my Jewish identity a spiritual meaning and purpose.

If not a genius, Dean Slonimsky could be content that he was at the very least like a beneficent genie, who by his spirit could transport me and many others to worlds we would never have known without his magical influence. Even though he is gone, the magic continues and I still inhabit those worlds to which he gave me entry. His memory, like a genie's lamp, can still be rubbed allowing the magic to continue and the worlds he created never to be lost.

18

In Spite of it all, Yes!

'Only the idea is real' was the declaration which began my education as a philosopher at New York University, Washington Square College in the Autumn of 1954. For the first time since I was eleven years old, I was going to school with Gentiles. Of course, NYU had many Jews. Even the non-Jews had assimilated Jewish mannerisms through living alongside the large Jewish population of New York City. Nonetheless, it was a non-Jewish environment and value system. William Barrett, the Associate Professor of Philosophy, who uttered these words after writing the words 'idea' and 'real' in gigantic letters on the blackboard, could not have been more of a Wasp. He was tall with big feet, wore Harris Tweed jackets from Brook Brothers and walked across the lecturer's platform with the confidence that he was the personification of American culture at its best.

'Only the idea was real'. How could this be true when the two were always perceived as opposites? According to Socrates and Plato, it was obvious, but it would require William Barrett to teach us the logic of this absurdity. 'What is this?' he asked as he pointed to his table. 'It's a table, but how do you know it is a table? Because, it is a surface standing on legs. Now you could not have known that it was a table unless you had the idea of table, of a surface which stands on legs. Without the idea of it, the table could not exist. It is the idea of 'table' which gives the table its reality. Therefore, only the ideal table is real and each physical table is only a reflection of this ideal. What ignoramuses call the Real World is only a shadow of what is really real, the World of Ideas'.

This was truly fantastic. This was more than a classroom.

It was a magician's studio and the philosopher was the magician. The table I was looking at was not real but the image of table in my head was real. If this was not magic, what was? Listening to that first lecture, I concluded that the real reason Socrates was sentenced to drink the hemlock was not because he was corrupting the youth, but because his logic was driving the Athenians crazy. What better way is there, when your own arguments are too weak for your opponents, than to wipe them out? It was mad, but I loved it. Henceforth, William Barrett was to be the star attraction at NYU.

Strangely enough, Barrett was not a philosopher of the Idealist school, nor was he a Rationalist. Quite the opposite, he was an Existentialist. He affirmed the brute reality of existence and did not believe that any closed idealistic system could protect the individual from the need to make choices and the consequences of not making them. But because he was a lover of ideas, which is how I would define an intellectual, he could teach any philosopher with sympathy and appreciation. Like Henry Slonimsky, whatever he taught, he ended up teaching himself.

I determined to enrol in whatever course William Barrett was giving, and at the beginning of each of my four college years, I looked with eagerness at the catalogue with this objective in mind. There was one very exciting course on the Philosophy of Modern Literature. T. S. Eliot and James Joyce were the authors under study. Barrett, however, was a spontaneous spirit and even before giving the course on T. S. Eliot, he walked into class one fine spring morning, strode on to the slightly elevated platform and started declaiming: April is the cruellest month . . . He recited the first five lines of T.S. Eliot's poem, *The Wasteland*, a poem with which I was not familiar when William Barrett caused these lines to resonate through the air waves. That day, I bought *The Complete Works of T.S. Eliot* and read them voraciously.

During my Freshman year, I was the youngest in the class, as Majors in Philosophy did not take courses in this subject until their sophomore year. For some reason, I was allowed to do so. My relative youth and inexperience was to cause me great embarrassment when during the second term we read T.S. Eliot's the *Love Song of J Alfred Prufrock*. We were discussing those lines, supposedly spoken by the woman after love making, 'This is not what I meant at all, this is not it at all'. Perhaps it was the confidence I felt after receiving the highest grade in a class of thirty- five students: an A- in the Plato course, which made me stupid enough to raise my hand and ask a rhetorical question, 'Why could not people take sex for what it was?' William Barrett looked at me nonplussed. The pretty girl sitting next to me turned around in shock. I understood their looks of disbelief only later when I too learn that the performance of the sexual act could be the most frustrating emotional experience when there is an alienation between two minds in love. Any sensitive soul would know this, unless it belonged to a virginal body, for whom the physical act itself is of the greatest significance because it is yet to be accomplished. Instinctively I felt that I had revealed myself either as a clot, which I was not, or a virgin which I was. I survived this experience but the memory was so embarrassing that I have blocked the response to my question and to this day I can only see, in my mind's eye, the surprised look on Barratt's face and the condescending smile spreading across the pretty face of my neighbour.

While he never spoke about contemporary events, I had the impression that William Barrett was a disenchanted liberal. I was too young to be disenchanted but I did feel politically cheated. The Second World War ended with victory against the most pernicious power that ever existed; but it was brought about by the horrendous dropping by my own country of two atomic bombs that demolished two cities, something which could only fill one with shame. The unbelievable revelation of what the country of Bach and Kant had done to millions of human beings; the realisation of the betrayal of Karl Marx's utopian dream by Stalin; the Cold War between East and West; the stalemate at the end of the Korean war; the breast beating of former Communists as they betrayed their friends under the pressure of Senator McCarthy in the name of a God-fearing and freedom-loving America left my generation with no political cause or social purpose. True, Martin Luther King was beginning to give the Civil Rights movement teeth, but it would still be some years before he would catch hold of the imagination of white youths. I envied the idealism and the intellectual debates concerning the achievement of a better world, in which my older brother had been engaged, before the bitter truth emerged that no political party or system had truth or integrity.

There was a clutching at straws. There was the Wallace campaign for the Presidency in 1948, which ended in abysmal failure. There was Paul Robeson singing his songs for a more equal America before I entered my teens. There was Adlai Stevenson, the sensitive and cultured orator with holes in the soles of his shoes who made us intellectuals hope that we could have a sympathetic spirit in the White House. Instead we got a general for President, who decided that the country would do best if John Foster Dulles ran the country's foreign policy while he played golf.

It was a period of confusion, fear and shame. The victory over the fascism and racism of the Axis powers left no sense of exhilaration. The behaviour of the Allies, e.g. Dresden, Hiroshima, Nagasaki, their passive cooperation in the slaughter of the Jews and other minorities; the carving up of new spheres of influence, between the U.S.A. and the U.S.S.R.; the Russian repression of the nationalist spirit of Hungary and Czechoslovakia all combined to give the postwar world a sense of hopelessness. Even the establishment of the United Nations was no more than the attempt to give five Powers the right to rule the world, if they could ever agree on an issue. Individuals felt powerless to change their world, and so they turned to improving their own personal situation. Those who were frustrated by the elevation of success to the highest pinnacle in the scale of values became rebels without a cause.

As an eighteen-year-old I was not aware of my political

frustration; I now know that it was there. I remember, after one class with William Barrett, joining him and some of my classmates in the elevator as it descended to the ground floor. He said, 'Perhaps this is taking us to the basement where we will be unloaded and sent to Siberia'. It was a funny fantasy or nightmare but it revealed our sense of unease with the political situation.

It was during my Freshman or Sophomore year that an Irish-American friend and I went to see the first American production of Becket's *Waiting for Godot* in an off Broadway theatre. I was riveted by the stark and sterile stage setting, the two bums , one looking into his hat for some new ideas, the other looking into his shoes for 'street' wisdom and finding only a bad smell, while they waited for the god who never came. The play spoke to me and I was taken aback when at the curtain call, my friend rose in anger and shouted: 'phoney, phoney!' For me, however, it was the clearest expression of the modern situation. The intellectuals could come up with no new earth-shaking ideas to bring salvation, and the ordinary man in the street was not a noble beast. Without a God in whom he could believe, without a cause and a hero to bear on his shoulders, the shoes of Everyman would continue to stink. The history of humanity also gave no hope, as we could never learn from it, and it was the blind leading the blind.

I trace my cynical attitude to politics to the generation in which I was born. Ten years earlier or ten years later, I may have been different. What saved me from total cynicism was my hunger and love for relationships and the strange kind of security given to me by my Jewish roots. Over the years I had met enough people who were kind and caring, I had learnt from enough teachers who spoke their truths very eloquently and I had a tradition of heroes whose words and lives proved that there was meaning in the universe. Soon, also, I was to experience first love, and this, had not all else been sufficient, would have made me, like Molly Bloom at the conclusion of James Joyce's masterpiece, Ulysses, say to life, not once, not twice but ten times – YES!

19

'Young Brichto, you must be in Love!'

First love was both a miracle and a revelation. The first because I did not believe it was possible. The second because the joy and sense of mystical unity which it gave me was incomprehensible. As a tenant of a body which embarrassed me since early childhood, I was physically ashamed and could hardly imagine myself unclothed in the presence of anyone but a doctor. Holding my own body in contempt, I could only but assume that any woman would feel the same. Sex for me was not a forbidden fruit, only unobtainable. While in late adolescence I had engaged in some love play, I found that it was I who was doing all the work, with very little reciprocal effort on the part of my female partners. In my late teens I had begun to despair of my capacity for inspiring love and physical and spiritual union.

Had I been born a Christian, I could have made my abstinence into a virtue. I could have joined the Catholic priesthood and decry the pleasures of the flesh, because I was not to enjoy them myself. Had I been a Hindu or Buddhist I could have led the life of an ascetic on the pretext that all pleasures turn to ashes in the mouth and the way to Nirvana was to kill the human appetites. I could have sought an idealistic cause to which to sacrifice my own needs. For me that would have been easy. I would have had a head start on Ghandi as I was skeletal even before going on an orange juice diet. I could have forgotten I had a body, or at the very least boasted of its insignificance and neglect as a sign of moral virtue.

But this was not the case. I desperately wanted love. I needed physical contact if I were to come fully alive. My ego required some compensation for its years of non-physical existence. Reinforcing my needs was my Jewish background. The first biblical commandment to Adam was be fruitful and multiply. It was considered sinful not to marry. My Zaydeh had married for a fourth time proving his assent to the biblical and rabbinic dictum, 'That it is not good for man to live alone'. As a child I had read biblical tales full of love and passion. Jacob moved boulders because of his love for Rachel. The unfulfilled lust of Potiphar's wife for Joseph brings him imprisonment and then elevation in the Pharaoh's court. I read of the seduction of Dinah and the revenge wreaked by her brothers upon the seducer and the entire city of Shehem. The tale of David's love for Bathsheba, his adultery and murder of her husband Uriah and the fact that he remained God's favourite, the ancestor of the Messiah, filled me with wonder. The rape of Tamar, David's daughter, by her half brother Amnon filled me with horror. But in all my biblical readings there was no condemnation of sex; only of those who allowed their lust, their jealousy or anger to lead them into the crime of lust.

I was able to sublimate my sexual frustration and thwarted desire for love by reading the Bible. The prophets often compared God's love for Israel to a husband's love for his wife, and God's anger against Israel as that of a hurt and aggrieved husband for a woman who in her prosperity had forgotten him and turned into a promiscuous whore, selling her wares to foreign gods. *The Song of Songs* attributed to King Solomon in his youth was the most erotic poetry I had ever read. What could be more sensual than these verses:

A garden locked up is my sister, my bride;
A spring sealed shut up, a fountain secured
Your body gives off the fragrances of an orchard of pome-
    granates.
With smells of precious fruits;
Henna with spikenard plants,

Spikenard as well as saffron, calamus and cinnamon
With all trees of frankincense;
Myrrh and aloes, with all rare spices.
You art a fountain of gardens,
A well of living waters,
And flowing streams from Lebanon.
Awake, O north wind;
And come, wind of the south;
Blow upon my garden,
That its smells may flow out.
Let my beloved enter into his garden,
And taste his precious fruits.
Ah, I have entered into my garden, my sister, my bride;
I have gathered my myrrh with my spice;
I have eaten my honeycomb with my honey;
I have drunk my wine with my milk.
Eat, O friends
Drink, drink deeply, all you lovers.*

I would memorise the verses in Hebrew and sing the
Israeli love songs with lyrics from *The Song of Songs*. My
study of the Talmud indicated no difference in attitudes
towards sex between biblical and rabbinic heroes. It was the
great martyr Akiba who declared, during a debate on
whether *The Song of Songs* should be included in scripture,
'All the Writings of the Canon are Holy, but the Song of
Songs is the Holy of Holies'. The fact that traditional commentaries interpreted the declarations of love to be between
God and Israel, and not between a man and a woman did
not in any way weaken the affect of the sensuality, but only
reinforced my belief that the sexual human relationship was
seen as the best parallel for the covenant between God and
Israel.

Another great Sage, Abaye, is reported in the Talmud to

* The translation is my own from *The Song of Songs, The People's Bible*
(Sinclair-Stevenson).

have followed a young couple early one morning into the country to prevent them from sinning. At a crossroad they parted with a kiss and a fond farewell. The rabbi returned to the village and leaned against a wall and wept declaring, 'Had I been that young man, she would not have gotten away so lightly'. He is consoled by an old man, 'Do not castigate yourself for your desires, for the greater the man the greater is his evil inclination'.

With my own need for love and physical contact, and the Jewish tradition that the sexual urge is a sign of strength, there was no way for me to find a saintly way out. But blessed be those who wait, whether impatiently or not. First love came my way. This is not the time for me to speak of she who brought first love to me on its wings. Suffice it to say that I was totally loved by a very special person. While I never believed, as do Orthodox Jews, in bodily resurrection after death, I thanked God for the experience of the spiritual resurrection of my body while I was still alive. My enjoyment of sensual pleasure made me feel that I had lost my blindness. I could see for the first time the joy of the flesh and the beautiful texture of life. As a convert often becomes more religious than those born into a faith, so did I become more dedicated to sensual pleasures because I had always been deprived of them and never believed that the deprivation would cease. I learnt that the flesh is innocent and pure. It is the mind that either makes it bloom or corrupts it or allows it to wither.

My first reciprocated love was mystical because my body, being loved, joined itself to my soul; my soul found happiness in the home in which it had been born. I became a whole being never again to be ashamed. The nature of love being what it is, in the imagery of *The Song of Songs*, my first love became my fountain of living waters, and in my own mind my skinny legs became tree trunks because she loved them. I brought to that romance all I had stored up in me for two decades. I shared all I had learnt. Quotations from the Song of Songs, the poems of John Donne, rabbinic writings, all the books I had read came trippingly off my tongue to give expression to every moment of bliss.

However unique was my own experience, romantic love is always madness. For days, weeks and months, I was in euphoria. An unfortunate separation did not abate my passion, but only increased the romance. With the surge of increased confidence, I thought all was possible. I volunteered to deliver the sermon in Chapel, a regular Friday morning ordeal when rabbinic students, usually of the advanced classes, preached and were criticized mercilessly by senior lecturers for their efforts. I was no more than twenty and had no reason for subjecting myself to such a trial, but I felt invulnerable. I chose a verse from Psalms as my text. King David says, '*V'ani tefiloh*', and I am prayer. I no longer have a copy of the sermon but my theme was that it was not enough to pray but each person must become a prayer. I finished the sermon, prepared for the best and the worst and got them both. John J Tepfer, a British expatriate and lecturer in Mishna and rabbinic sources, looked at me and said, 'Young Brichto, you must be in love. Have a nice weekend!'

A story told about Akiba is one of my favourites. He saw the wife of the tyrannical Roman Governor Turnus Rufus. He spat, he laughed and he wept. He spat because such a beautiful creature had her origins, like all human beings, in a drop of semen. He laughed because he foresaw that she would become his wife. He wept that such a beauty would one day turn to dust. First love gave me laughter, gave me new life and in gratitude made me say as did Rabban Gamaliel, whenever he saw a beautiful woman, 'How wonderful are your works, O Lord'.

20

Two Spies in the Camp

Finally, I was ready for the big fight. Painstakingly, at the age of seventeen, I worked my way through *The Brothers Karamazov*. I identified most strongly with Alyosha, the believer, who saw good in everyone. He was also, like me, the baby in the family. This was rather far fetched as I did not feel that I had the beautiful innocence of Alyosha nor his religious faith.

The identification of my brother Chanan with Ivan, the sceptic was more realistic. As Ivan was Alyosha's teacher in the brute realities of life, Chanan fulfilled this same function in my life. I sought to identify my middle brother Zvi with Dmitri, the spontaneous worshipper of life, women and song, who while he would not harm a fly, was strong enough to kill a bull. Except for his good and fun loving nature, the connection between the two was very tenuous.

You could well ask, as I do now, why had I the need to make any such comparisons. I can only surmise that this was one way of increasing my security by finding a pattern for my existence in a greater scenario than my own limited world. It also made me feel less lonely, as by these identifications I was able to join myself more fully into the romantic adventure of three brothers struggling to liberate themselves from their Russian background.

There was also an element of arrogance at work. If the Karamazov family was important, so was mine. There was the picture of my bearded Zaydeh's torso over the mantelpiece in the living room, looking most profound. He had given me a genealogy which proved beyond doubt that our illustrious ancestry included the great medieval commentator

Rashi, and that we were descendents of King David. With such a background I had to be important and my life had to have more meaning than my surroundings and situation suggested. This arrogance would be obnoxious in an adult, but in an adolescent it could be understood and forgiven as a yearning for place – and the recognition that this small speck was of some significance in an infinite and frightening universe.

Chanan was my mentor in life. Like Ivan, he questioned everything and taught me to do the same. He was a cynic, but like Diogenes the founder of that movement, a seeker after truth, even when it was soul destroying. Chanan seemed to see through people and situations. But while he was hard-headed, he possessed a core of softer sentiment which enabled him to enjoy the goodness of life. Ivan Karamazov, reflecting the darker intellect of Dostoevsky and his own violent background, shows no such sentiment. Life is an unredeemable veil of tears. God is dead and all is permitted and men drench the earth in each others blood. No Messianic Age could make up for the suffering of one child, no less the millions of innocents who have been violated and murdered throughout the history of mankind. Ivan spoke for all the sensitive atheists of the world, for whom the positing of omnipotent beneficent being who would tolerate such human horrors is the greatest blasphemy against the divine spirit. Chanan,, however, was saved from bitterness by the taste of a good glass of wine, the juiciness of a perfectly grilled piece of steak, the embrace of a grandchild and yes, the discovery of new meaning in a biblical text: shades of my Zaydeh!

Chanan made two decisions which proved to me that, unlike Ivan, he had not given up faith in the potential goodness of life. He married Milly. Surely his association with a woman who saw every bit of goodness as a sign of God's benevolence, and every bit of evil as a god-given opportunity for good people to improve the world revealed his own faith in life. He also became a rabbi. By doing this, he both cast his lot in with the angels and joined generations of Jews who have by their actions and prayers affirmed their faith in the ultimate victory of truth over falsehood and good over evil.

While Chanan was helping me to shape my future, he allowed me to share in the development of his own present. This reciprocity strengthened the bond between us, giving me a sense of equality with him which removing any traces of resentment, which I would have felt had I only received without being able to give in return. I was on several occasions invited to join him and Milly when they went up to visit his weekend congregation in Monroe, upstate New York. Chanan gave me his sermons to read, and I took as much pleasure in the praise he received after delivering them as he did. It was sheer joy for me to sing folk songs with Chanan and Milly as we drove up to Monroe, and equal joy, when after Friday evening services, I was invited to join them and a favourite couple from the congregation for waffles, pancakes and coffee at the Roadside Diner near Route 17.

One Sermon my brother delivered had a great influence upon me, not so much because of the content but by the circumstances surrounding its composition. Chanan had returned from serving as a Chaplain in Korea. He had decided to become a biblical scholar and, while preparing for his doctoral studies, he had taken on two part time jobs, one of which was to be the Rabbi of the newly founded Reform synagogue in Englewood, New Jersey, the other was Dean of the School of Sacred Music of the Hebrew Union College in N.Y.C. I was then eighteen and just beginning college.

It was the Eve of Yom Kippur, the Day of Atonement. Chanan conducted services in a rented Church and was very depressed at its conclusion. The large Church with its dark wooden arched beams made the service cold, and he was disappointed with his sermon. He had given into the demands of the Officers and made his sermon into an emotional appeal for financial support for Israel. He felt that he had cheated the congregation and himself by not giving a spiritual and intellectual message. By the time he arrived home, he was disconsolate, feeling that he had to make it up to himself and his congregation by delivering a powerful and moving address the next morning. The sermon that he had prepared was good but no longer good enough. He determined to write a new one on the holiest night of the Jewish Year.

I would never have questioned his right to work on the Sabbath of Sabbaths, but he felt the need to justify his action to himself so he explained that his obligation to inspire his flock took precedence in the scale of religious values over his breaking of the commandment of not working. He would have to write into the wee hours of the morning if he was to create a masterpiece. In this he reminded me of those Hasidic rabbis who would break laws in order to be true to their spiritual instincts.

God must have approved. The sermon was completed by 4:00 am. That morning he delivered 'The Four Fates', a beautifully poetic sermon in which he compared, favourably of course, Judaism to Christianity, Islam and Buddhism. The message was that it was Judaism alone which affirmed life and man's freedom to determine his own future. It was beautifully illustrated with quotations and tales. He quoted Omar Khayyam. He told the story of the appointment with Death at Samara. He ended dramatically with the sentence, 'For Judaism, Man has no fate, he has only a destiny'. It was wonderful! I wanted to jump up and applaud. My God, he had done it. It was like the joy of Professor Higgins when Liza Dolittle had properly said the 'Rain in Spain falls mainly on the plain'. Chanan was pleased with himself and Milly and I thrilled in his glory as member after member indicated their approval.

It was then that I appreciated the enormous pleasure that one could receive from creative writing especially when there was the immediate feedback obtained when you were delivering your own creation . 'Great sermon, Rabbi', was a statement that offered the kind of pleasure received when giving birth to a beautiful baby. Perhaps, that's why the

proper expression is to 'deliver' a sermon and not to 'give' it.
It is in the reception of the 'delivery' which gives pleasure
both to the giver and the receiver.

That Yom Kippur must have influenced my decision to
become a rabbi. My brother had already suggested that I
should keep the options open and had persuaded the Hebrew
Union College to allow me to take courses in the rabbinical
postgraduate department while doing undergraduate work at
New York University. Before I could take courses, however,
I had to be admitted as a rabbinical student. This entailed
an interview before five faculty members and an exam in
Hebrew. This double ordeal increased the likelihood of my
slipping into the rabbinate, because what was the point of
suffering possible rejection unless you intended to take
advantage of acceptance. The exam presented little difficulty:
the interview was different. I felt very inferior. Most of the
students at the Hebrew Union College had degrees. Many
had had other careers before switching to rabbinical studies.
The Admissions Board, therefore, was interviewing students
between the ages of twenty three and thirty five years. They
looked at me, an awkward stripling of eighteen. In their eyes,
I saw confusion. They had the task of being objective in spite
of the fact that I was Chanan's brother.

To make the right decision was their problem. I had my
own. I wasn't sure that I wanted to be a rabbi. Nor was I
certain that it was intellectually honest to become a rabbi. My
faith in God was weak, though my attachment to Judaism
very strong. That was all right for Jewish laymen, but more
should be expected of a religious leader. What if they asked
me whether I believed in God? I discussed this moral
dilemma with Chanan. He told me not to worry and com-
forted me by telling me of an Admissions interview when
Henry Slonimsky was Dean. One Professor had asked the
applicant that very question, 'Do you believe in God?' The
poor fellow had no chance to answer as the Dean shouted,
'Now what kind of question is that to ask!' It sounded reason-
able enough to me to ask such a question of a person wishing

TWO SPIES IN THE CAMP

to be a rabbi. I was not asked that question nor do I remember the interview except that it was all rather laid back with a few weak jokes to put me and them at their ease. I left the room feeling that I would be accepted but more out of sympathy than on my own merit.

Attending classes both at NYU and HUC at the same time made me realise how much more comfortable I was in a Jewish environment. HUC appeared to be a perfect compromise between the Western World and my Zaydeh's world. There was respect for knowledge, the belief in the superiority of Judaism, but also the scientific spirit which was not afraid of questioning even the most basic traditional assumptions. The lecturers had been schooled not only in their Jewish subjects but in secular universities. Also, there were non-Jews: one, who was quite remarkable, who taught speech and elocution. For the first time in my life, I felt intellectually at peace with myself.

There was still the possibility that I could make academia my career, as I loved philosophy and teaching, but one semester in a post graduate scholarship at NYU changed my mind. The courses were dry and uninspiring. I was bored by the logic and formal philosophic concepts which we were studying. There were only a handful of students in the different classes and the interesting philosophy lecturers were not teaching, for one reason or another. There was no personal tuition and I felt less part of an ivory tower than an intellectual wasteland. I stopped attending classes and did not register for the second semester. A few months later my absence was noticed, not by the lecturers but by the administration, which sent me a note drawing it to notice my that, as I had not registered and was not attending classes, I could no longer be regarded as a student. I considered that a fitting logical conclusion to any ambitions I had to be a professor of philosophy. Of course there were still other options. It was suggested that I could be a journalist. I enjoyed writing and showed some skill as an essayist. I did not act on this because I felt comfortable at rabbinical college, too much so to be stimulated to research the possibilities of a career in journalism.

Now, I would attribute my decision to become a rabbi to my desire to remain a Jewish Jew. Had I gone for another profession, I could imagine myself drifting away from Judaism as a result of other interests and pressures. A rabbi can be a bad person: after all he is only human. There is nothing to prevent him from being a philanderer, so long as he does not get caught, or from playing golf on Yom Kippur, though he wont be able to tell anyone if he scores a hole in one. But at the very least, observant or non-observant, moral or immoral, one thing is for certain: a Rabbi cannot escape his Jewishness. However much I rebelled against orthodoxy, I loved my Jewish background and becoming a rabbi was a decision to put my Jewish identity into an irreversible situation. Had I not done this, I could see myself as a two-day-a-year Jew boasting to my rabbi that my Zaydeh was a rabbi and that my ancestors were great scholars. He would reply politely, as I do now, 'Really, how interesting' but thinking, 'How often have I heard this before?' In view of this, it is ironic that in order to rationalise and justify this decision I had to resolve two issues: on the one hand, the Zaydeh and Abah would be shattered by my decision. By becoming a Reform rabbi, I would be confirming my heresy, and not only that, but I was going to be teaching it to others. I would be *hoteh oo machtee*, a sinner and one who caused others to sin. My father would prefer a non-practising orthodox son who was a doctor to a son who was a rabbi who was practicing the wrong Judaism. By becoming a Reform rabbi I would be causing him and the Zaydeh public embarrassment. On the other hand, was my faith strong enough even to be a Reform rabbi? Would not my questioning spirit prevent me from giving my congregation the security they required to maintain their belief in Judaism.

I resolved the first issue by selfishly declaring that it was my life and not theirs, and that whether they knew it or not, I was affirming the Jewish background my Zaydeh and

Abah had given me by choosing the rabbinate. I rationalised the second on the basis that, in Judaism, action not faith was the essence, and that our religion was more concerned with what God demanded of humanity than the nature of his reality. As a rabbi, I would follow in the tradition of those Hassidic rabbis who had, because of the human suffering, constantly questioned God's justice. Dean Henry Slonimsky made the decision easier because he taught that the Jewish God, The-Holy-One-Blessed-be-He, was a God who only grew in power as his greatest creation, Man, grew in goodness.

The Zaydeh accepted my decision more easily than my father. I don't know what happened, but I soon discovered that he had persuaded himself that both Chanan and I were infiltrators in the Reform movement, that we had only become rabbis in order to bring Jews closer to true Judaism, and not to the Reform heresy. His love for us both was too deep to allow him to believe that we could betray him. So it was that I was to become one of the Zaydeh's two spies in the camp. Strangely enough, while this had never been my intention when I chose the rabbinate, the effect was in fact to bring my Zaydeh's world closer to that of the Jews I led and made them join me in the journey around my Zaydeh.

21

'Don't worry, Rabbi, one day you will get a congregation'

In 1956, my brother offered me the opportunity to make $350 by conducting High Holy Day Services in Clearfield, Pennsylvania. I had just turned twenty and was still a kid. I never really learnt how to say 'no' so I agreed and worried the whole summer on how I would cope. There were about thirty Jewish families in the town and only one synagogue. Because they wanted to satisfy the more traditional, they celebrated the Jewish New Year for two days, which meant additional sermons. Also, there was no choir, so I would have to provide the singing myself..

I was teaching pre-rabbinic students Hebrew that summer in the country home of a former Ambassador to Siam. It was situated in the most beautiful part of upstate Pennsylvania. He had given his home to the Hebrew Union College with all its contents. It included treasures of Chinese carpets, carved furniture, images of Buddhas and Lohans in their hundreds, not to mention the models of ivory husked elephants which stood on wall ledges surrounding the spacious living room. It was an unbelievably lovely setting for study. Hills and valleys, the rich scent of summer was about everywhere. In my case it was particularly overwhelming. The pollen count was high and my asthma was worse there than anywhere else. It was as though the beauty of the place was killing me. In spite of the suffering, I returned several summers because it was a veritable paradise on earth.

That summer, I prepared myself by writing my first sermon. The biblical reading for the New Year was my theme. It was the binding and near sacrifice of Isaac. I contrasted Abraham's response to God's test with that of Adam's after he has eaten the forbidden fruit. Abraham says *'Hineni'*, here am I. Adam hides from his master. God asks, *'Ah-yeh-koh'*, Where are you?' and Adam replies, 'I hid because I was afraid'. In my sermon I explained why they reacted as they did, and whether, as we entered the New Year, we were like Adam or Abraham. Every sermon should have a moving story and I found a lovely Hasidic tale in which the rabbi is asked how it is possible for God not to know the whereabouts of Adam. The answer is that the question that God asks of Adam, he asks of every man and woman. 'Where are you and where are you?' It is a metaphysical question to which even God does not know the answer. This was the task of the Jewish Day of Judgement, for each Jew to look at himself.

Armed with my sermon and three old ones of my brother, I got off the train at Clearfield Station, and after waiting an hour to be picked up discovered that I had arrived a day too early. It was not that I did not know when the Jewish New Year began. I was told by the College authorities that they expected me a day earlier but the leaders of the congregation were never told.. The additional day with nothing to do only increased my nervousness. I practiced the readings and the musical pieces. I was trembling even then.

When the time to perform finally came, I could not believe the extent of my nervousness. My opening prayer in English was so garbled and incomprehensible that I hoped the congregation thought I was reading Hebrew. How I stumbled through that first evening service, I do not know, but whether time heals or not, it certainly passes, and the service came to a merciful end. An hour before the morning service I swallowed two valiums. I stumbled over the first paragraphs but eventually found my feet. My lack of confidence was due to several factors, my youth, my inexperience and my humility. What right had I, a lad less than twenty, to lead Jews in worship on the holiest days of the Jewish calendar?

Had I been an officer of the congregation, I would have
sent me packing, but they thanked me. On my return to New
York City, my brother consoled me. 'Sidney, you don't know
who conducted services last year. In comparison, you may
have been terrific, and remember you have many years ahead
of you should you decide to become a rabbi'. I decided to
bury my Clearfield experience in my sub-conscious and start
afresh.

I gave the following year a miss. In two years, I regained a
measure of confidence. My legs always trembled, and I had
difficulty in getting the first sentence out of my mouth but I
began to enjoy the power that performers have in keeping the
attention of their audiences and the praise that follows. I also
showed my enjoyment. This helped. 'Rabbi', they would say
to me, 'It's so nice to see how much you enjoy yourself up
there'. Judaism had never been a lugubrious affair for me, so
why should being a rabbi make it any different? As I grew in
confidence, I threw myself into the joy of exhibitionism. I
smiled at individuals if they caught my eye. I turned my
youth and insignificant physique into a virtue, as I used them
both to gain sympathy and understanding. During the High
Holy Days, when I wore a white rabbinic robe, I was told that
I looked like an angel.

When I was a full rabbinic student, I was given a trial
for a regular weekend congregation. That meant activities
throughout the weekend; Services as well as Religion School
on Sunday morning. It was New City, New York. After the
service a fellow came up to me and said, 'I liked your sermon,
where did you get it from?' I told him that I had written it.
'Really', he said, 'I thought you got them out of books'. I am
still not sure he believed me, but I was flattered that he
thought it good enough to have been stolen. The congregation hired me. Every Friday evening, I would be entertained
for the evening meal when the host and hostess prided
themselves on the quality and amount of food and the choice
of wines. Sometimes, or too often, I was polite, accepted a
second helping and another glass of wine and by the time I

came to the service I felt bloated and euphoric. Not only did I appreciate the drowsy faces in the congregation, I could have fallen asleep myself, had I not been leading the service.

This was a period when rabbis were 'regular guys'. They would drink and tell jokes with the best of them. I had no difficulty following that pattern. When the brandy was served with coffee, and it was a Remy Martin, I would smile approvingly. My pre-dinner drink was always a dry martini, and we would joke about how dry it ought to be, and whether the lemon peel should be dropped into the glass or just wiped over the brim of the glass. The up-and- coming executives liked my style and I showed great interest in their work. I was very popular.

It was not long before I learnt how one displeased person could affect a rabbi's life. I had been told that the decision to give me the job was unanimous. How was it then that towards the beginning of summer when re-appointments were made, I was told that they were looking for someone else. Furious, I questioned my closest friends in the congregation. Well, under pressure the truth came out. It was *not* a unanimous decision to appoint me. One person opposed me, and that happened to be the Chairman. He was upset because during the interview, I had offered my belief that God was as unhappy at the death of a child as were we, and that the challenge given to men was to gain the wisdom to prevent premature deaths. It seems that the Chairman had had a child who died and had been consoled by the belief in divine providence.

He had never told me of our theological difference, but instead chose to chip away at my credibility. One evening when I suffered through a service, having made a great effort to get to the congregation in spite of a bout with oncoming flu, he told the congregants that my sudden departure for home following the service was because I was woozy from too much drink. I was prepared to challenge the decision, but I had the offer of a far better position in the Bronx.

The congregation made me a lovely farewell lunch and I

shattered them with my address. Unbeknownst to them, I knew, because my middle brother worked in the leather department of Saks Fifth Avenue, that they had bought me a leather attaché case because my name was inscribed on it. I came fully prepared, expressed surprise and delight at the lovely case and then went on to deliver an 'extemporaneous' speech on how useful it would be for carrying my sneakers and sandwiches. I went on for ten minutes, only pausing for the laughter. 'Rabbi, you ought to be in show business', was the crowning praise of my ministry in New City.

The normal praise for a rabbi was 'I did enjoy your sermon'. It was apparent that the function of the minister was more to entertain more to teach. The philosopher Kierkegaard recognised this over a hundred years ago. He noted that once people went to the theatre to be entertained and the church to be edified, but now they go to church to be entertained and the theatre to be edified. When television entered the competition for people's attention, it is not surprising that rabbis and ministers had to make greater efforts to hold on to their flocks.

My congregation in the Bronx posed two other challenges. The *Bimah*, the platform, was within fifty yards of the Bronx Elevator. The trains would come by every twelve minutes, and ten seconds would have to be allowed for it to pass because nothing could be heard until it did. If your timing was good and your sermon short, you could miss it. If not, you had to hope that your address was sufficiently interesting so that they didn't forget what you were talking about during the rattling of the trains wheels. The other challenge was how to maintain one's neutrality without being considered a coward by the two synagogue factions: one group which was prepared to go into massive debt in order to move and the other which felt that the congregation could not afford to move at such an unreasonable cost. Both factions were at each other's throats. My guide and mentor was Sam Pinkowitz, a Vice President of the Chase Manhattan Bank who sold currency forward. He helped me to be a moderating force.

Both in New City and the Bronx, I met several individuals who inspired me by their goodness and courage. It has been my experience in all my congregations to find that there was at least one person who had more religious faith or moral strength than myself. My first funeral was of a seven year old child who had died of leukaemia. I had visited her in hospital and had seen her body fall away while her spirit became even more angelic. On the way to the cemetery, the father drove and I was in the car with his wife and his two other children. He laughed as he went over a big bump and reminded the children of how their sister had loved it when he went quickly over high gradients in the road. She would want us to laugh, he said. This man who was large and masculine had developed signals which he made with his hands to indicate to his wife that he loved her even when they could not speak. I think that I said the right words during my eulogy because some woman fan of mine came up to me after the service and said, 'Sidney, when I die I want you to do my funeral'. I was so flummoxed that the words which came out were not really appropriate, because politely I replied, 'Molly, it will be my pleasure'.

I tried hard to be a good student rabbi. I poured out every bit of knowledge that was in me. It was probably too much for them. Jewish theology and philosophy, Jewish history and heroism, Jewish lore and legend had become my life and I expected too much when I wanted them to be as thrilled as I was by the riches of my heritage. It was with amazement that I saw people did not remain behind for my talk and discussions following those services when we had adult education. They always had a good excuse, but the fact is that home was more attractive than any wisdom or learning that I could impart to them. All this, the bravery of people living with death, the disinterest of congregants in my teaching combined to teach me lessons in humility.

What I found always incredible in my relationships to my congregations was that even as I grew older, I appeared to myself to be a youngster in comparison to my congregants.

My superior knowledge did not give me any sense of superiority or status. 'You look just like a Bar-mitzvah up there', was one flattering comment. I did not mind this because I was not comfortable with the authority bestowed upon me by the rabbinate. I shied away from it because I did not feel that I was more religious or had more faith than other Jews. The major difference between me and them was that I had made Judaism my life and they had not. It was my job to teach them how lucky they were, all the evidence withstanding, to be Jews. This could only be done if Judaism was made exciting and not boring, with smiles not frowns, with a light touch rather than a heavy hand, with the emphasis on joy and not guilt.

Because of this attitude and the friendship I exuded, I appeared as youthful as my years. When I had come to England after my ordination, and three years later had been appointed to the prestigious position of Executive Vice President and Director of the national Liberal Jewish Movement, I was from time to time in that capacity, invited to guest preach at the Liberal Jewish Synagogue in St John's Wood. On one such occasion, following the service at *kiddush*, when the blessings over wine and bread are recited, one older member asked me which congregation was mine. As Director, I served no particular synagogue, so I told her that I didn't have a congregation. She looked at me sympathetically, touched my arm and said, 'Don't worry, one day you will get a congregation'. She gave me a smile of encouragement, took the glass of wine and walked away.

22

Praise the Lord, I have been rejected!

Being the fountainhead of the American Reform Movement, which sought to achieve a balance between Americanism and Judaism, the Hebrew Union College expected its rabbinic graduates to serve their country. Its Board of Governors looked askance at those individuals who had entered rabbinic training primarily to avoid the military draft. In my student days, it was a condition of acceptance to the HUC that we would volunteer to become chaplains in the US Armed Forces after graduation.

In my final year, therefore, I painfully but dutifully offered my rabbinic services to the US Army. I did not look forward to spending three years in the Army, even though the Korean war, in which my brother had served as a Chaplain, was over and there was no potential danger. I would be safe, but the joy of wearing a Second Lieutenant's uniform was little consolation for I would be wearing it on some military base in the backwaters of Missouri or on the bleak plains of Texas.

There was one hurdle, as far as the army was concerned, and one chance as perceived by me, to escape the wearing of khaki and that was the 'physical'. I was hoping that my history of asthma might disqualify me. Unfortunately, my examination was in early March when the pollen count was almost non-existent, my breathing was normal with no hacking or wheezing. I had heard that allergies were no bar to passing the medical. My brother, who had bad hay fever, though without asthmatic symptoms, was proof of this. He had even had a rheumatic heart as an infant, and they still accepted him!

The day came. I arrived and was shown into a small room

in which I was asked to strip. I did so, and when no doctor came, I decided to take matters into my own hands. I opened the window wide and breathed in the cold drafts. A healthier person would have been exhilarated. In my case, by the time the doctor entered the room, I was in a state of breathlessness and shivering. From the look on his face I could tell that even before he put the stethoscope to my chest, he was not impressed by the human specimen trembling before him.

A letter arrived from Frederick O Hunt Jr, chaplain (Major) USA Personnel and Ecclesiastical Relations, future Chief of Chaplains of the Department of Defence. I read:

> 'We regret to inform you that the determination has been made that you do not meet the physical standards of appointment in the Chaplain Branch, US Army Reserve, and active duty. In view of the foregoing, we must decline your offer of service.' Your interest in the Army Chaplaincy is sincerely appreciated. We regret that this action is necessary'.

Whoopie! Once again in my life, I had reason to rejoice in my inferiority. As I put this letter down, I thought that I had discovered a new secret of life: human strengths can let you down because they can falter, but weaknesses are far more reliable especially if they are helped along.

Surely this was an opportunity not to be missed. Three years of life returned to me. For the last year of my rabbinic studies, I had heard talk among my colleagues of positions on offer, assistantships, University chaplains, one-man ministries in smaller congregations, and more talk on the perks and the advantages of the job. The vision of entering this career world was almost as horrific as that of joining the Army. I had the uneasy feeling that the beginning of my rabbinical career was already a spiritual dead end. Whatever appointment I accepted, I would be looking for the next upward move. It appeared incongruous that the acceptance of a position in the name of God and Judaism was to be viewed not for its intrinsic value of teaching God's word and ministering to his children, but only as the first stepping stone towards a successful, well paid and prestigious rabbinic career.

As a student I once attended the annual convention of the Central Conference of American Rabbis, and all I heard in the corridors was the comparisons of salaries and the internal struggle of rabbis with their lay officers. The younger rabbis looked up in awe at colleagues in large and rich congregations. They tried to unravel the secret of success, if it was not the pure good luck of having their senior rabbi die prematurely with them ready to bounce into the saint's well-worn shoes. Amidst all the theological debates and sacra-political resolutions at the Convention, the young novices were looking for prospects of promotion, the middle aged contemplating whether they had reached the end of the success line and should be consoling themselves with a good pension, and the successful of all ages walking around with the look that they had at the very least inherited the best of this world, if not the next.

Was this for me? No, it was not. I acted quickly. In April of 1961 I was rejected by the US Army. In the same month I had achieved a letter from Dr Julius Levy, Chairman of the Committee of Graduate Students of the Hebrew Union College, offering me a Graduate Fellowship in the amount of $3,000. The next month, Professor Stein of the Hebrew Department of University College London informed me that I had been accepted as a post- graduate student in Hebrew and Aramaic. The following month, Dr Leslie Edgar, Senior Minister of the Liberal Jewish synagogue offered me a part-time assistantship for £1,000 a year. I had escaped the Rabbinic rat race as well as the American army and with an income exceeding £2000. 'Olde England, London Town, here I come!' I had come of age.

23

The end and the beginning of
the matter

Often I hear others and indeed myself saying in regard to
a person: 'I cannot figure him out'. I realize now that there
must be those who would say the same of me. This is
not surprising as I too was not able to figure myself out until
I wrote these biographical essays. Indeed, I had never given
the inconsistencies in my behaviour any consideration. I
assumed that in any given situation, I was acting on instinct,
based perhaps on some lessons from experience as to the
likely outcome of my actions. Now, I think I understand
the apparent contradictions in the way I relate to events
and people.

For example, reacting on my own to a happening, I will
respond intellectually. 'How could so-and-so have done
this?' I will ask and then set off on a course of action, an angry
letter, or a call for a meeting to set the matter right. I will
be quite confrontational, demanding change and improve-
ments. As soon as I meet the 'erring' individual, however, I
find myself identifying with the other person's situation and
I will seek a reconciliation.

The exploration of my formative years yields an explanation for this polarity in my personality. Because of the need
to survive by my wits and not by my muscles, because excitement was only possible for me in the world of ideas, I have
always enjoyed a good moral or intellectual battle. My adrenalin flows when I read a stupid article, or hear an offensive
statement. I rise to the challenge, send off a letter to the
Times or run to the telephone to rally the forces. These

responses are similar to that of the little child of nine who expressed his individuality by protesting against his teacher's political prejudice. I enjoy the consequences of my action, relish the response and the cut and thrust of debate. It makes me feel alive, no doubt in the same way a soccer player feels when he has been part of a team effort which leads to a goal. But as soon as the game has been played, I seek a conclusion. My love of reconciliation stems from my love of diplomacy, the art of making the difficult possible. I find my formerly belligerent self saying, 'Well perhaps it was a failure of communication, a misunderstanding of intent'. In this phase, I see the adolescent making peace with the Yeshiva High School's Registrar over 'Hobo Day'.

When I am on my own, I well up in anger against the opposition. In a personal confrontation with opponents, however, I seek peace and a return to good fellowship. This could be the consequence of a deep insecurity in my childhood. My desire both to make an impression on my environment and the need to be loved and appreciated is my explanation for these contradictions.

The desire for independence and individual fulfilment also explains my need to lead and my refusal to throw myself totally into any cause, even if it be the worthiest. Such utter dedication leads me to a loss of self. However much I love my people and my faith, I have to confess I love myself more. It is not that I say, 'What's in it for me?', but more like, 'This cause is me but not *all* of me'. I love Judaism, but not so much as to allow other Jews to pay me less than I deserve, as I devote myself to giving their children a Jewish faith. I consider myself a Jewish patriot. I have made Jewish history *my* history, but not so much that I have gone to be a pioneer in Israel, because living in Israel would not enable me to meet other personal needs. I do not believe in sacrifice, but in free will offerings which enrich me while, hopefully, enriching others.

I like to think that my love of self has led me to appreciate that 'What is right for me may not be right for others'. When individuals come to me for advice about their future, I always ask, 'What do you want? What will make you happy?' I encourage them to accept that their first duty is to themselves. Polonius, being an old wag, did not get it totally right when he said, that if you were true to yourself, you could not be false to any man. You can be true to yourself and still cheat and hurt others but at least you know what you are doing and not deceiving yourself. If one sacrifices oneself for others, all will end up suffering when hidden resentment and anger rise to the surface. I am not speaking of love relationships where the distinction between persons are often confused because of the sense of oneness between lovers.

The paragon of rabbinic sages, Hillel, said it most succinctly: 'If I am not for myself who will be?' If I am secure in my own love of self, I can freely love others. If I look after myself and loved ones, I will expect others to act identically. My love of individual independence and pluralism is another reason why I hate those 'isms' which seek to solve social problems in the naive faith that one theory can apply to all individuals. The human factor is forgotten. In the end it is the individual that counts. A good teacher can successfully teach his subject, regardless of the pedagogic system he employs. A poor teacher using the best methods will still fail.

I have to confess that I am not as moral as I would like to be. Honesty does not come naturally to me. I have to struggle for it within me. It is not automatic for example for me to return too much change but requires a conscious decision. There are times in my past when I have discovered later that I was given too much change and did not bother to return to rectify the matter. Was it my mother switching price tags on ties in a department store? Was it being laughed at for returning the change which came gratuitously out of the telephone box? Was it the fact that my father never told me the importance of being honest and the self respect that comes with total integrity? If he did not tell me, it may have been because he did not tell me very much on any subject or assumed as he assumed about everything else that honesty was to be expected from me. Of course, I would never steal, so why talk of honesty? I am certain it would have helped me had the importance of this virtue been discussed.

As to loving and being loved, I have partially overcome the lack of physical affection in my childhood. I believe that I am affectionate but feel that because I received so little as child, I tend to hold back. Yet, that emotional expression means very much to me. Whenever I see a touching scene of reconciliation or joy between parents and children, I cannot restrain the tears which well up in my eyes. I pretend I am sneezing to excuse bringing my handkerchief to my face, but I fool no one. It is as though I myself want to live through the experiences which I watch on television or see on the cinema screen. It is a sad commentary on real life that one sees so few moments in real life which make one weep. My happiest moments are when I experience uninhibited joy in the faces of members of my family, or experience a moment of total unity with them.

I wish I could be more expressive of my love in ordinary times as well as in times of crisis. I know how important it is and that love unexpressed is love repressed and the shallower because of it. I find myself often quoting the verse from the Midrash, 'Not only did God love Israel but so much did he love her that he told her he loved her'.

Finally I must return to my Zaydeh, the source of my Jewishness. Hillel also said, 'If I am only for myself, what am I?' If I have given my life to my people, it is because in the Jewish people and the teachings which make up its soul, that I find my identity and my security. When I struggle for Jewish survival I struggle for my own. Strangely enough, not being especially favoured by nature, except in some intelligence, my life appears to me as a microcosm of the history of the Jewish people. Survival has not been easy, nor can it be taken for granted. As I read of refusal of my people to die but to love life and to thank God for it, I see the mirror of my own life.

Would it have been the same had I been born a frail

creature in another minority culture? I do not know. What I do know is that there is so much in Jewish lore and learning, so much in my holy books and history to which I could associate, from which I could learn and which made me proud to be a Jew. Judaism was my only inheritance and I made the most of it.

My deep involvement in Jewish life has made me very secure in the company of non-Jews. Because I chose both the *Sforim* and the Western classics, and because I knew from my study of Jewish history, that Jews assimilated the best of the cultures in which they lived, I decided to do the same. Knowing my roots, loving the world of my Zaydeh, and being secure in it, and knowing that it was always there to return to, the great cultures and religions of the West never threatened me. Ecclesiastes, concluding his philosophical work wrote:

> Beyond this my disciples be warned
> There is no limit to the making of books . . .
> The end of the matter, all things being considered,
> Fear God and keep his commandments
> This is the duty of all mankind.

I would say, as I finish this book, that the end of the matter is that it is people and not theories which shape our lives. I have been fortunate that many have gracefully touched my life and their touch has enhanced it. My Zaydeh may have been the first, but he was not the last. He did however set the standard, and he made me respond gratefully to any human creature who offered me love, understanding or wisdom. My brother Chanan used to laugh at me as a growing adolescent when I joyfully accepted a drink, 'One thing about Sidney, he never says no'. This was true then, it has been true since I crossed the sea to England to start my adult life in earnest. It is still true, and I shall die happy, if someone offers me something to which I will be able to say in my dying breath, 'Yes'.

Epilogue

It is vanity to set out to write about oneself and to expect others to read what one has written. It is humbling when one comes to the end of the story because of the discoveries made on the way. The effect is a paradox, pointing to the truth of the rabbinic explanation of why a person has two pockets: so that in the one he should have the words 'For me was the world created' and in the other the words, 'Remember that you are but dust and ashes'.

Glossary of Hebrew and Yiddish words

Aliyah, pl. aliyot	the honour of being called up to say a blessing before a reading from the Torah
Am haratzim	ignorant people
Bimah	synagogue platform
Derasha	rabbinic discourse
Din	a Jewish law
Dreidel	a gambling top played on Purim
Quitlach	a Jewish 'blackjack' card game
Erev Shabbat	Sabbath eve
Goldena	a golden
Homentashen	cake with poppy seed filling in the appearance of a hat as a reminder of the arch-villain Haman in the book of Esther
Kaddish	prayer in memory of the dead
Kashrut	dietary regulations
Kibbud av	show of respect for one's father
Bikkur cholim	the mitsva of visiting the ill
Kibbud tzibbur	public modesty
Kiddush	blessing over Sabbath or Festival Wine
Krechs	a Jewish moan
Mazal tov	good luck; 'mazal' means constellation; 'tov' – good
Medinah	state or country
Mensch, pl. menschen	a man, i.e. a decent human being
Minyan	ten adult Jewish males
Mitsva, pl. mitsvot	Jewish commandment, obligation, also a good deed, also an honour
Olam habah	the world-to-come
P'kuach nefesh	the mitsva of saving a life
Rav	a rabbi or distinguished person
Rebbeh	head of Hassidic community or teacher in a yeshiva
Rosh Hashanah	the Jewish New Year.
Schwartzeh	a black person
Sefer Torah, pl. sifray Torah	scroll of the Five Books of Moses
Sforim	books, scholarly works
Sh'co-ach	congratulations on achievement
Shochet, pl. shochtim	a Jewish ritual slaughterer
Shul	synagogue
Sukkah	wooden booth used during festival of Tabernacles
Tarfut	non-kosher food
Tfillin	Phylacteries; black boxes, containing scriptural portions, to be attached to a man's left arm and forehead during morning prayers excepting the Sabbath
Yarmelka, kapul	skull-cap
Yeshiva	a rabbinical seminary; school for Jewish studies, esp. the Talmud
Yordim pl. of yered	emigrant-one who goes down from the Holy Land